THE
NEXT
CENTURY

DAVID HALBERSTAM

THE NEXT CENTURY

AVON BOOKS ◆ NEW YORK

A leatherbound signed first edition of this book has been privately printed by the Easton Press.

AVON BOOKS
A division of
The Hearst Corporation
1350 Avenue of the Americas
New York, New York 10019

The William Morrow and Company edition contains the following Library of Congress Cataloging in Publication Data:

Halberstam, David.
    The next century / by David Halberstam.
        p.   cm.
    1. World politics—1989-   2. Twenty-first century—Forecasts.
    I. Title.
    D860.H35   1990   90-46188
    303.49′09′05—dc20   CIP

First Avon Books Trade Printing: February 1992

AVON TRADEMARK REG. U.S. PAT. OFF. AND IN OTHER COUNTRIES, MARCA REGISTRADA, HECHO EN U.S.A.

Printed in the U.S.A.

OPM   10 9 8 7 6 5 4 3 2 1

For Harrison Salisbury

THE NEXT CENTURY

I

ON FEBRUARY 26, 1989, I WAS one of two speakers before the governors of the fifty states of the Union. It was a memorable occasion, not merely because of the distinguished audience but also because Henry Kissinger was the other speaker. There he was, well tanned, surrounded by what seemed to be several bodyguards, and looking a little less chubby than he does in his photos. The governors were eager to hear him, for he was to talk about the new, ever more startling events taking place in the Soviet Union. This, then, was not just some abstract speech; this was a speech by one of the most celebrated men of our time on a subject that, in our shrinking world, pressed close to them and their America.

For the first ten minutes or so he really had them. He performed with considerable charm and in the beginning with a great deal of self-deprecating humor. As he started to talk about Gorbachev, their interest was further piqued. They sensed that what was happening in the Soviet Union was the beginning of something historic. If there was any hope for their America, however long-range, it was that there might be a lessening of

East-West tensions, which might in turn permit a reevaluation of national priorities, which might eventually result in a redirection of our nation's political, emotional, and economic energies. The phrase "peace dividend," implying those vast billions that might be used for domestic needs, had not yet become part of the political lexicon, but that was when the idea of a major break in the Cold War was but a glimmer.

It was still relatively early in the Gorbachev Revolution, before the Soviet premier had helped pull the plugs on the various puppet regimes of Eastern Europe. However, by then the Soviets had unilaterally pulled their troops back from Afghanistan. It was clear that something that represented a radical departure from Soviet policies and rhetoric of the past was taking place in Moscow. Just two weeks earlier I had sat in a meeting with Barbara Tuchman, the esteemed American historian, and she had said in the most casual way that the events taking place in the Soviet Union were the most important ones in her lifetime.

Kissinger was having none of it. He was condescending about what Gorbachev was doing, and he was even more condescending about those poor Americans who were taking it all so seriously. His theme was simple: Not only should we be wary of Gorbachev, but if there was any great weakness to American policy during the entire postwar era, it was American naiveté, our belief that we could make deals on a personal level with a succession of Soviet leaders. According to him, only the Nixon-Kissinger team had remained immune to this temptation. He made no mention of the Soviet withdrawal from Afghanistan. His speech struck me then (and even more so today) as the last speech of the old order.

I sat three seats away, facing the governors, and I watched their reaction. As Kissinger continued to hammer away with his Cold-War rhetoric, they began to lose interest. The governors are today, I think, quite possibly our best public servants. The better and more experienced ones are well ahead of their counterparts in the Congress in sensing where this country is and where it is headed; one of the ironic outcomes of the Reagan Revolution, with its greatly diminished federal aid to the states, is that it forced state governments, however reluctantly, to become better and more accountable. The senators and members of the House of Representatives live in Washington, where the aura (and the pleasures and the perks) of hegemony still linger; by contrast the governors must live more closely with the realities of posthegemony America. If their states lose factories, they are the ones faced with declining tax bases and less money with which to prepare their citizens for new kinds of work. Congressmen are the ones who speak out on the danger of too much Japanese investment in America; governors are the ones who go hat in hand to Tokyo, begging Japanese firms to locate in their states. What are political abstractions on the floor of the House or Senate are realities in state budgets. In the governors' world, politics are closely tied to economics, which has become vastly more important in America in the last ten years.

This, then, was a fascinating scene unfolding in front of me: Kissinger, Nobel laureate, a symbolic figure of the old America, with its marvelous weapons systems, its dominant role among the superpowers, standing in front of these less celebrated public servants, who had to cope with brutal budgets, expanding social needs, deteriorating infrastructures, and public service institutions that often seem overwhelmed by the pressures they faced. America, I thought, meet America.

Even as he finished and left with his entourage, I changed my speech. Generally that year my speeches shared a common theme: the correlation between Japan's (and Korea's) primacy in education and their industrial success (and conversely, the correlation between low test scores and lack of productivity and economic health). Instead, somewhat to my own surprise, I spoke about national security.

I said that most of the people talking about national security in this country were ill equipped to do so because they had lost touch with the country, that national security was no longer an index of weaponry (essentially a missile and tank count), if it ever really was, but a broad array of factors reflecting the general state of national well-being. It included the ability of a country to house its people, to feed them, to educate them, to provide them with opportunities in keeping with their desires and education, and to instill in them trust and optimism that their lives were going to be valued and fruitful. Those in Washington were so fascinated with realpolitik and weaponry that they tended to forget that the just and harmonious society was, in the long run, also the strong society.

Other than in its ability to produce military hardware, the Soviet Union had failed miserably. Its great disease was universal cynicism and pessimism. I did not think I was naive about Gorbachev. I did not think that he was pushed by love of freedom as we in the West define it, but I was sure that he was pushed by love of country. His own shrewd, extremely contemporary conclusion (in contrast with those of the geriatric leadership that had preceded him) was that the system from which they and he had so richly benefited was strangling the country.

He was most assuredly a modern man, I suggested, and therefore, he had to know that in terms of economic efficiency the Soviet Union was no longer merely behind the United States, Western Europe, and Japan but in danger of falling behind such emerging countries as South Korea. Moreover, the gap in technology and science between the Soviet Union and its competitors was steadily widening, and this had profound consequences not merely in economic terms but in military ones as well. The high-water mark of the Soviet Union's power probably came in the early sixties at the time of the Cuban missile crisis, when it could manufacture large amounts of traditional, albeit relatively primitive weaponry. This, and the very size of its vast land armies, seemed to substantiate its claim to being a great power. It had been in decline ever since because its economy had not kept up. Or to put it differently, given modern military machinery's dependence upon computers, can a vast country like the Soviet Union, so obsessed by the need for secrecy that it has been afraid of a Xerox machine, let alone widespread use of computers, continue to be a great power? Modern technology demands computers, but computers are not merely instruments of science and warfare; they are instruments of communication as well. Can the Soviets have the former without the latter?

We should, I suggested, take no pleasure from the unveiling of the self-evident weaknesses of the Soviets. They were neither our model nor a model for anyone in the future, although for too long we have justified our weaknesses by comparing ourselves with them. In fact, our competition with them long obscured ever more serious vulnerabilities in our society. For the first time in America we were in danger of falling behind as well. Compared with the Soviets', our system and our economy looked dazzling; compared with others' now just beginning to hit their strides, we were beginning to look tired and worn. If there was any purely economic model for the future, it was the Japanese. They were a fierce and relentless competitor; it was now quite possible that they were setting the standards for other nations in terms of being a well-educated, industrious, disciplined society.

We were, I suggested, already entering the next century, and it was our not very secret secret that the American Century was over as well. "The Cold War is over," says Chalmers Johnson, one of our most talented Japanologists; "the Japanese

15

won." Soviet communism, which dominated our thoughts and our politics for more than forty years, was suddenly no longer a menace. After World War II our sudden, almost unnatural affluence had allowed us to proceed with the all-encompassing dynamic of the Cold War and to carry the burden almost alone.

At the same time it was finally the grinding nature of the Cold War that began to exhaust us and our economy, which eventually in no small part made us vulnerable to competitors less burdened by the myth of empire. Our economy began to show significant signs of being less productive and less competitive than it had been in the fifties and mid-sixties. The economic assumption of the postwar years that whatever it was commercially, the Americans did it best was no longer true. Even more worrisome, our educational system was seriously malfunctioning. We were producing a generation of young people ill equipped to deal with a complicated and challenging future. The governors, I noted, were in a good position to know if America was going to be a great power in the years 2010 and 2020 because they knew the quality of our average high school graduates far better than did the people in our national security complex.

A day in February 1990 seemed to mark the convergence of these two strands of the postwar era: NATO and Warsaw Pact ministers met in Canada and gave permission for the reunification of Germany. On the same day Drexel Burnham, the financial house that did much to keep the illusion of the American Century alive for an extra decade by substituting for true productivity the deft manipulation of junk bonds, went bankrupt. Mostly, though, the indicators of American malaise do not make the news. On occasion an event like the sale of Rockefeller Center to the Japanese jars Americans, but far more serious signs go largely unnoticed—for example, the decision of a consortium of American high technology companies, called U.S. Memories, to call it quits in mid-January 1990. The consortium was formed to compete with the Japanese in the development of basic memory chips or DRAM. Though Congress had relaxed its antitrust laws to permit such groups to function, that which is natural for the Japanese, the ability at once to share and to compete in the same industry, turned out to be alien to us. We handed over the future of DRAM to Japan. It was a story that barely made the network news. A film clip of a consortium not consorting is not very exciting.

Now I think back to that afternoon with the governors. Like others, I am still stunned by the events from Eastern Europe and Moscow that flooded television screens every day as the Soviet satellites broke free. Events outstrip the projections of even the most knowledgeable experts. One thinks of Emerson's line lightly adapted, "Events are in the saddle, and ride mankind." Never has that seemed more true. Above all else, I think about how Kissinger was wrong in his talk about the great shifts of history: Gorbachev *is* history, or as the Soviet leader himself said, warning the East Germans to move with the new tide before it was too late, "History punishes those who come late to it."

II

THE SOVIET EMPIRE UNRAVELS BEFORE our eyes, if indeed empire it ever was; Gorbachev gives away what once would have been called chips without receiving in return any chips from us. He does it to lighten his nation's burden. His top financial advisers complain angrily to their American colleagues how heavy the burden of responsibility was for them in Eastern Europe. "Can you believe that we spent—absolutely wasted— between twenty and twenty-five billion dollars on Eastern Europe since World War Two, providing them with a military umbrella and selling them oil below market rates?" one such adviser told an American. "You Americans thought we were imprisoning them, and then we looked around one day and found that we got no benefits and that we were the prisoners."

Empire, it seems in the modern era, burdens. Why? I suspect it has to do with modern communications, which make oppressed people more aware of their conditions, thereby making it harder to subjugate them. It is increasingly difficult to censor thought in an age of sophisticated electronic media. Modern communications inevitably define modern conscience and speed across national borders. The oppressed can call attention not merely to the inequities that colonial or neocolonial powers inflict but also to the price of such tyranny. That is why in both the French Indochina War and the Algerian War the French generals believed that they had been undermined by the French press, and that is why General William Westmoreland still goes around telling everyone who will listen that he never lost a battle but was undone by the politicians and the press at home. In the Soviet Union, where the press was more successfully controlled, there was a less immediate sense of what the Soviet Empire did to its people and to those of its satellite nations, but it was always there in the form of passive resistance (and, on occasion, open resistance in the East European nations). The final Soviet venture into imperialism, in Afghanistan, culminated not merely in the active resistance of Afghan rebels but in the increasing willingness of the Soviet press to write about it.

It is not just that traditional forms of totalitarianism failed but that they failed in what I would call the Orwellian dimension—that is, with the state using modern technology (particularly television) as an instrument of political and psychological control. It never worked. Throughout Eastern Europe television was the property of the state. Real news might be broadcast by Radio Free Europe, but there was no underground machinery to compete with television. Yet state news was always seen for what it was: party propaganda, devoid of legitimacy. The underground news service, the Grandmother Radio Network, as it was known, was always more powerful.

John Darnton, one of *The New York Times* reporters who covered the early days of Solidarity, remembered that on the third day of the Solidarity strike the government flew a small plane over the Lenin Shipyard, and showered down thousands of leaflets. The leaflets reproduced the format of the local Party newspaper and announced that the workers had voted to go back to work. It was a moment right out of Orwell: using the media to tell people utter lies about their own decisions. But the reaction of the workers was merely unadulterated rage, and at this crucial moment, Darnton thought, that rage helped them gain strength and confidence.

We live in a wired world, and nothing reflected it better than the events of 1989, from Beijing to Eastern Europe.

The wired world is a recent phenomenon. As recent an event as the Korean War was still an old-fashioned story, distant and largely removed from the force of modern communications. Ed Murrow is properly remembered as the best broadcaster of his generation, but looking back, we see how conventional his much ballyhooed documentary on Korea was. A clip shows him talking to a soldier from Louisville, Kentucky. "When you look at that moon up there do you think of Louisville?" Murrow asks. The soldier seems to assent. "Who's your sweetheart?" Murrow asks next. "Would you like to say hello to her? . . ." Even in the early sixties, when I worked overseas, journalism still seemed rather traditional compared with the way it is today. Network news shows were only fifteen minutes long and broadcast in black and white. Satellites were not used to beam back stories instantaneously from distant countries. Television reporters sent back film by plane, much, in Sander Vanocur's phrase, like mailing overnight letters home.

Print reporters took significantly longer to file stories. One of the things I remember with pleasure about both the Congo (now Zaire) and Vietnam was that the communications were not as good as they were soon to become. I could reach Paris by telex instantly, but Paris could not reach me so easily. It could leave me a note, which I had the choice of either seeing or not seeing. For a reporter working at a newspaper of not inconsiderable bureaucracy, that was the essence of freedom.

Vietnam first reflected the wired world. It was, in Michael Arlen's phrase, the living room war. The Soviet Union, for all its seeming authoritarianism, was not immune to the changes in communication. It was becoming harder and harder to seal off an entire nation from the world. Détente, brief though it was, helped connect the Soviets. What Moscow got was economic help and wheat; what it lost was the capacity to keep its communications network entirely separate from that of the West. The Soviets were inevitably sucked into the broader community of nations from which they had been self-exiled. This made them at least partially dependent upon the West's economy and thus, gradually, reluctantly, but inevitably, dependent upon the West's good opinion.

In the seventies a handful of dissidents—most notably Solzhenitsyn, Sakharov, and Shcharansky—reached the entire world by their connections to a few distinguished American print reporters in Moscow. The situation in the late eighties represented a huge leap over that. We may debate, as I do, the proper uses of commercial television in America, but its impact upon events in Eastern Europe was dramatic: There is a sense that only television can project (as it did back in the early days of the civil rights movement and then again during the Vietnam protests), first, that there are clear moral choices and, second, that the whole world is watching. It greatly accelerates the cycle of events and on occasion makes ordinary people infinitely braver. In Eastern Europe the coming of American television was something that those who were rebelling understood and wanted. John Darnton and John Vinocur, who was also a *New York Times* reporter in the early days of Lech Wałesa's challenge at the Gdansk shipyards, remembered clearly when Wałesa and the men around him realized how big their audience was.

At the very start of the strike the workers were wary of

Western reporters. They would not give out their names, and if Western photographers or cameramen approached, the Polish strikers simply turned their backs. Then, on the third day, a remarkable thing began to happen. The news of developments inside the strike area quickly went out over the different Western news agencies and then an hour or two later came rocketing back over the BBC Radio bulletins that the workers could hear on their hand-held radios. The strikers, so long isolated in a totalitarian country, realized that despite the price they might have to pay later, they were connected to the wired world *and therefore, they were not alone.* A dramatic change took place. They no longer turned their backs to photographers and television cameramen. They began to give out their names to be used in stories. They learned how to give briefings. Vinocur was ushered into the small section the workers had barricaded to be Wałesa's office to meet the leader. He called it Wałesa's Sierra Maestra in his story. Darnton, arriving from Warsaw, introduced himself to one of the strikers and soon heard his name announced over the loudspeaker as if he were a powerful visiting dignitary. Both reporters noticed an increasing sophistication: Wałesa and the men around him quickly learned the pecking order of the media—who was important and who was less important—and how to ration their time.

Vinocur remembered two moments that showed how important a free press had become. The first occurred after a settlement favorable to the workers had been handed down earlier in the day. Word of their victory had been passed around, but the shipworkers refused to celebrate until it was announced over the radio (all the workers seemed to have Sony headsets). The second incident came when Vinocur went to the Polish airline office to buy his return ticket to the West. The young woman behind the Lot counter asked him if he was a journalist. He said yes. You are leaving us? she continued. He nodded his assent. "Don't go yet," she said. Why? he asked. "Because the longer you're here, the better for us," she said, and gave him his ticket.

As I write, Gorbachev, hero of the Western world for the first and most dramatic part of his rule—the withdrawal of the Soviet Empire from Central Europe—faces more difficult tasks: modernizing the Soviet Union, making coherent its hopeless economy, and galvanizing a sullen and unresponsive citizenry. His first accomplishments are probably gift enough to us; he has already changed not merely the face of Europe but, more important, the politics of the West. He is the most radical of modern leaders, breaking more rules than anyone else on the international stage because the rules in his nation were so regressive, so backward that they crushed not only its citizens (something the old ruling elite believed it could tolerate) but also the nation itself (something the new ruling elite understands it can no longer tolerate). If he is a man of the party and a man of the system, he is also, as the British journalist Martin Walker has noted, the representative of a new class in Soviet society. The first Soviet leader since Lenin to go to college, he reflects educational growth and social change. Raisa Gorbachev, educated as well as or better than he, was a philosophy professor and a participant in pioneering Soviet sociological studies. Their daughter is a doctor, and she is married to a surgeon. They are the quintessential Soviet modern upper-middle-class family, a reflection of a growing educated elite, sophisticated, traveled, privileged, proud. At this stage a central question to Gorbachev's leadership is: Can such people represent the Party?

What impresses me most about Gorbachev is something that goes beyond political systems and national boundaries: his immense pride and confidence, which drove him to take power

24

at so young an age. Our personal journeys mark us. The longer the journey, it seems to me, the greater the confidence of the man or woman who completes it. Gorbachev's personal journey from a childhood of overwhelming rural poverty is one of the longest for a Western leader in the postwar era. (Khrushchev, who gloried in his peasant origins, rose just as far.) For an American leader to come from so simple a background, one would have to go back a century. Gorbachev's confidence was born of that ascent, of having swept aside every obstacle in his way. En route he becomes the Communist world's first media superstar, and television becomes, to the surprise of not merely the West but the Russians as well, an instrument of Soviet political power. If Wałesa is the first Eastern European leader to connect to the wired world, then Gorbachev is the second. The media success comes easily; he is, after all, the first Soviet leader who does not hide from the camera. His strength on television is his confidence, his lack of fear of the communications process, his belief that he is good at it and has nothing to hide. We see his exuberant, almost brash delight in being unpredictable, and we are impressed.

If he seems to be the leader now dominating the world stage, he had, on his way to that position, to unlearn more than anyone else. His mind is, therefore, more open than most men who have come to power. He has become one of the most innovative world politicians of this century; comparisons are made with John Kennedy (and Raisa has been called the Soviet Jackie). But his surprises are far greater than Kennedy's. Kennedy used modern media so much more openly and skillfully than his predecessors (those televised live press conferences) that it was a quantum jump in politics as theater. Television was a brand-new instrument of his presidency. Moreover, in a world accustomed to such venerables as Eisenhower, Churchill, de Gaulle, Adenauer, and Macmillan, he was young, the first

25

leader cast forward after the most terrible of wars, and therefore his very youth seemed to offer hope. Aside from his image, though, his politics were essentially conventional. Gorbachev is different. He is completely unorthodox. He has been cast forward by a system of politics that we in the West have rightfully considered the most stagnant and regressive of the postwar era. That it has produced the most inventive and flexible of modern leaders is what is so intriguing.

The first stage of Gorbachev—his apprenticeship—went largely unnoticed in the West. As a loyal apparatchik he worked his way up through the bureaucracy for some twenty-five years. He was a dutiful Stalinist as a young man and was jarred by Khrushchev's denunciation of Stalin; as Zdenek Mlynar, the Czech liberal who was Gorbachev's roommate in college, told David Remnick of *The Washington Post,* "like everyone else at the time he was a Stalinist. In order to be a true reforming Communist you have to have been a true Stalinist."

Stage two of his career was a stunningly quick rise to power. He became a protégé of Yuri Andropov, a Spartan, knowledgeable, worldly figure and the leader of an immensely powerful faction in the Kremlin, the anti-Brezhnev faction. To be a member of the Andropov group was to know all that was wrong with the system and, even more important, to know that it did not work. If there has been a gradual change in Gorbachev's personal vision, it has been, I suspect, the growing (and probably grudging) acceptance of the idea that one cannot ventilate a society economically unless it is ventilated politically as well. That makes him the most daring tightrope walker of all time, the authoritarian ruler trying to undo some aspects of an authoritarian system, while trying to stay in power.

As he first took over after Andropov's (and Chernenko's) short reign, there was tentative talk of modernizing, of *perestroika* and *glasnost.* One had the sense that he might be different in some way from those who had gone before and that he seemed restless with the past and the condition of his country. Finally it became apparent he was knocking seriously on the door to the West with the unilateral withdrawal from Afghanistan.

The third stage was Gorbachev the Liberator, for which modern media dubbed him Gorby (or Super Gorby). He was the darling of the Western media, in fact, more popular in the West than in his own country. Polls on occasion even showed him more popular in America than many American politicians. The honeymoon period lasted about six months, from late 1989 into the early spring of 1990. If anything, his biggest mistake was to raise such high expectations both at home and abroad.

That leads us to stage four. It is a harsh and frustrating time for him. At home he seems to get little credit for his deeds abroad, and he is charged with failing to improve the quality of life. The various national republics, taking seriously what he has done on his western boundary, talk openly of independence. His reforms open up his country to far more penetrating journalism than in the past, both on the part of foreigners and, more important, for him, on the part of Soviet journalists. He begins to learn the hard way, as other heads of state have learned before him, that being a part of the wired world is a two-sided proposition. (One thinks of Lyndon Johnson, loving his absolute access to the media in the early days of the Vietnam War, when his acolytes, unchallenged, were on television every night; and then Lyndon Johnson coming to hate television when such correspondents as Morley Safer and Jack Laurence began to demonstrate the independent power of the media.) Certainly the early images of Gorbachev as a young and vital general secretary added greatly to his power at home and abroad. As he made an impact on ordinary citizens of the West, so he increased his leverage with its leaders; and as he succeeded in the West, so he strengthened his hand in internal Soviet politics.

But at the same time his course has opened up the Soviet Union, almost overnight, to a kind of scrutiny it has never seen previously. American television networks now give out hand-held video cameras to stringers throughout the country (an act that would have been considered espionage only a few months earlier). My friend Jim Laurie, the ABC correspondent in Moscow, films a simple but devastating piece on how an ordinary Russian family shops for food in Moscow—how long it takes and how little you get. At one supermarket he and his team are filming when the manager comes out to tell them they must stop. In the old days there would have been a finality to that order. But now it is different. All the other shoppers in the store rush over to Laurie's defense. "Let him film," one of the Muscovites shouts. "Let the world see how little we have!" The manager hastily retreats.

Suddenly it becomes Gorbachev's task, under the unsparing deadlines imposed by the Western media, to revitalize a system that has been moribund for some seventy years. (No wonder he, like a long series of American Presidents before him, vastly prefers dealing with foreign affairs; when you make an executive decision in foreign policy, it is carried out, or at least it appears to be.) Under this ferocious new scrutiny, Western eyes fall for the first time on Soviet weakness, and Gorbachev is blamed. Magazines that only a few weeks ago fought hard for the chance to have an exclusive interview with him (always with their editor in chief and Moscow bureau chief pictured with him) now bear his photo on the cover again, this time the portrait slightly more dour, bearing captions like "Gorby: Can He Survive?" or "After Gorbachev." *Newsweek* publishes a cartoon of him alongside Hitler and Napoleon as "famous dictators who bogged down in the Russian countryside."

Gorby the Liberator is quickly forgotten. There is talk of a society undergoing implosion, and one writer envisions a Soviet Weimar, the most terrifying suggestion of all. Americans who always worried about the Soviet leadership's being too strong find themselves in the unaccustomed position of worrying about a leader who may be too weak. On the eve of his Summit with Bush in June 1990 the Western media proclaims that Gorbachev has arrived holding the weakest hand of any Soviet leader since the war. The White House, hearing of Yeltsin's maneuvering in Moscow, moves to shore up its new friend and deliberately leaks details of Yeltsin's crude behavior when he was in America. Like LBJ, Gorbachev, first the beneficiary of the modern media, becomes irate with their instant judgments (instant judgments no longer so favorable). He summons a number of top Soviet journalists and angrily berates them for failing to understand the vast amount of good he has done for their country and for being insufficiently *grateful*.

In the spring of 1990 my wife, Jean, and I went to Moscow as part of a writers' group to fraternize with Soviet writers, though this kind of project rarely works well, and this particular trip works less well than most. Many of the Russian writers and journalists we would like to meet have been notified only at the last minute or not at all; in general, there seems to be a great schism within the Writers' Union with the result that many of the younger writers simply do not go to the Writers' Club. That gives us ample time to wander around Moscow. It is my first time here, but I come with certain preconceived notions. As a junior at Harvard I took Government 115, Professor Merle Fainsod's course, the title of which was something like "The Authoritarian Forms of Government in the Soviet Union," but more popularly known in those days as "Know Your Enemy." In the ensuing years as a correspondent in Eastern Europe I came to regard the Soviet Union as a formidable place, clumsy but powerful. Particularly to the countries I was covering it seemed an all-powerful and threatening place.

One feared the Soviet Union, had a certain contempt for it, but in the end grudgingly respected it. Its leaders seemed to exude ominous power: Stalin, ever-secretive, hiding from public view in the Kremlin; later Khrushchev, barreling around the world, wildly aggressive, filled with a kind of animal vitality, determined to show that he was, in fact, the peasant as head of state. He even seemed to glory in how badly his clothes fit. Let Macmillan be beautifully tailored, he seemed to be saying; it was one more sign of England's decline. Then there was Brezhnev. I remember when he visited Poland in 1965, short and bulky, a caricature of a first secretary, delighting in the official rounds that his Polish hosts had arranged for him and their obedience to him. The faces of the Polish people, who had been turned out, were cool and strained, their smiles forced; the faces of the Polish officialdom were hollow, faces made of wax. That was power; these people were his subjects.

As I stood in Red Square this past spring, I wondered at how those images had disappeared so quickly. Here was the Soviet Union reduced sadly to the reality of itself. Everything was worse, much worse than I expected: The people are sullen; the bureaucracy heavy. The stores are as empty as we have heard, though people ride in a hundred to two hundred miles every day from the countryside because their own regions have so little food that even Moscow with its virtually empty stores seems preferable. By the time we leave, people who shop in Moscow are ordered to show proof that they are Muscovites. I have no doubt that shoppers will get around this, that there will be some black-market tariff that they can pay, as they have gotten around so many other orders and obstacles. I am stunned by the extent of the black market and the degree to which the nation's own currency, the ruble, is scorned and the dollar is prized. I was bitterly chastised by one cabdriver for not having quite the right amount of dollars and for offering to pay him in Finnish marks, a hard currency. *Finnsky?* he said, pouring out contempt.

One is told about farm machinery rusting away because a small repair cannot be managed or even about deliberate sabotage of equipment that probably never worked anyway. The worst stories are always about the distribution system. It is ironic that the most centralized of societies is, in terms of goods, the least centralized. We hear of thousands of acres of fresh produce harvested, taken to a railhead and put in non-refrigerated cars, which are then placed on a siding and quickly forgotten, only to be remembered when the foul odors begin to seep out from the railroad cars. By one estimate some 50 percent of the produce grown never makes it to market for such reasons. What Russia needs most of all, an American friend of mine who does financial deals here tells me, is for the entire country to be taken over by Federal Express. My friend has been talking to a very high Soviet official, one of Gorbachev's closest financial advisers, who has suggested that the West Germans, in order to speed the process of German unification (and to make sure that Germany remains in NATO), will offer the Russians a loan of some $3 billion. A few weeks later there is official confirmation of the story. The Soviet official, rather than being pleased, is appalled. This kind of windfall is what the Soviet Union needs least, he says: "We will waste it all. We lack the capacity to absorb it. It will all rot away the way we function now." Then he adds: "You can classify Russians three ways—first, by nationality, second, by religion, and third, by degree of corruption." Earlier that day the Russian had gone before a meeting of Western bankers and talked with open bitterness about his people: "If in the West your neighbor has a

31

better house than yours, then you work harder in order to have as good a house as he does. But here in Russia your reaction is different: What you want to do is burn his down."

I expected to find some of the same qualities among the Russians that I had encountered in the people of Eastern Europe: the bonding of people by dint of their hatred of a system imposed on them, a sense now of heady optimism because the system may finally be changing. But the differences are striking. In Eastern Europe there was always the sense of an occupation imposed from the outside, of ordinary trying to make the best of a bad situation, and therefore, by and large, of not going out of your way to inflict pain on your fellow citizens. People tried to share what little they had. The symbol of that on a national scale, it seemed to me, was Janos Kádár, after he took over Hungary in 1956; his mission seemed to be to make the Hungarian condition as bearable as possible under obviously cruel conditions, to make sure that there was an acceptable level of food and consumer goods. A similar case may be made one day, I suspect, for General Wojciech Jaruzelski; no matter how he may have seemed to his own people and to Westerners in the early days after the crackdown on Solidarity, he, in fact, reflected a formidable strain of Polish nationalism.

The Russians struck me almost immediately as different. An ordinary person with even a meager amount of power took pleasure in wielding that power over someone else. Worse, people do not accept personal responsibility for their acts. Some twelve years ago my Polish friend Andrzej Wroblewski took his teenage son Tomasz on a vacation to Leningrad. Tomasz was not impressed. "Look at the people," he told his father after two days there. "In my knowledge of history the citizens of great empires were always very happy, and it was their subjects in the lands they colonized who were unhappy. But look at this empire and these people: *They* are unhappy, and *we* are unhappy."

32

When Soviet leaders talk about change in the Soviet Union, they know they are addressing something that is generational; there is, says one Russian writer, a good chance that those over twenty-five are already too far gone, too corrupted by entitlement on one hand (a low level of entitlement to be sure, but entitlement nonetheless) and cynicism on the other. There are daily reminders of this. On our first day in Moscow we have spent twelve hours making a long trip to what is alleged to be a "typical" Russian village in the countryside, in reality a sort of Russian Disneyland. It is ten-thirty at night. Jean and I are tired, and we want to eat in the main dining room of the Hotel Ukrainia. The maître d' has a half empty restaurant at her disposal, and many of the waiters seem to be taking prolonged cigarette breaks, but she obstinately refuses to seat us. If we were a group of four, she says, we could sit. But there is no room for a party of two. This byplay goes on for some twenty minutes. I think she believes we should go find the hard-currency restaurant, said to be elsewhere in the hotel, and spend our dollars there. But I am tired, and I feel obstinate. I have rubles, and I want to spend some of them. If not here, where? If not now, when? So far we have made little progress. I keep gesturing at the empty tables. She keeps shaking her head. Just then an interpreter from our trip walks by. He intercedes on our behalf with no success. His embarrassment is considerable. Finally I ask him to tell her that if she were in my country in a similar situation, she would be seated. No one would turn her away. Suddenly she comes alive, almost bitterly so. "That is because you Americans live in the twenty-first century, but we Russians live in the nineteenth century," she says so that we will understand not just her and this restaurant but this country. Her history lesson completed, she then seats us.

The Soviet officials may now choose to look at their intervention in Eastern Europe as benign, the good comrade taking care of his weaker, younger brothers, but the East Europeans will have none of it. To them it was always an occupation. The power of the colonizer was manifest in an army and in the immense powers of the secret police. They were encouraged to inform on one another. Talented men and women who did not espouse this week's doctrine were silenced professionally. The resistance that those nations offered was generally passive; they would make things fail. Periodically, though—the dates are interesting because it seemed to happen once every generation, or about every twelve years, in 1956, 1968, and 1980—it flared into open resistance.

In 1965, when I was a reporter in Warsaw, the *Times* asked me to write an essay on what twenty years of Soviet rule had accomplished in Poland, and in my audacity I wrote that it had accomplished nothing, that while there was an overwhelming Communist presence, nothing espoused by the regime had ever taken root. I was promptly called into the Foreign Ministry and expelled. But of course, it was true. So although it should come as no surprise that one day the old order exists, and then the next day it starts to collapse, as far as most Westerners are concerned, this is history fed by a secret subterranean spring. One day Lech Wałesa and his people are, if no longer in prison, the outcasts of the society, and the next day they win virtually every seat in a parliamentary election, and their colleague and trusted adviser is the prime minister of Poland. Lenin's statue comes down from the Gdansk shipbuilding factory, and his name comes off its wall. I go back to my files and find something Wałesa said in an interview at his lowest moment, after the Polish regime had crushed Solidarity. A reporter asked him about the future, and Wałesa, a devout Catholic, responded, "The Gospel says, 'Those who were humiliated will be lifted up.'"

Wałesa and his Solidarity more than anyone else exposed

the bankruptcy of the system. After all, there had been challenges to it for many years, but they had been the protests of intellectuals, students, or Jewish revisionists—all, by the standards of any Eastern European regime, untrustworthy and easy to ignore. What set the Solidarity protest apart was that it was the workers' protest in a workers' paradise. Wałesa was an unemployed electrician, a carpenter's son who was born after the War and only thirty-eight when he came to international fame. He had been kicked out of the Communist union earlier because he had dared put on the table at a meeting of high officials the grievances of his fellow workers; he made the mistake of believing that in a workers' paradise a worker should have rights. He had risen to power in 1980 during the strikes in the Gdansk shipyards, after trying to start his own non-Communist worker's movement. The success of Solidarity—within a year there were ten million members in a country with only thirty-five million people—underlined the failure of communism in Poland.

Theirs were not theoretical protests; they were the protests of men and women exhausted by a bankrupt system that was sucking them down with it. Day by day they dismantled the most important thing the government had: its facade of legitimacy. This cost the government dearly. A legitimate government does not lose face easily, but an insecure government with little in the way of indigenous roots takes its image very seriously. Jacek Kuron, one of Solidarity's most important intellectuals, once noted that the Polish government was so discredited that if it produced a golden egg, "first, the people would say it was not golden; second, that it was not an egg; and third that the government had stolen it."

In the end, Wałesa, Kuron, and others produced something remarkable: a broad-based, instinctive protest against a powerful totalitarian society. Crushing Solidarity in the end was the same as crushing the Polish people.

To the new generation of Soviet leaders preparing to come to power during the early eighties the events in Poland were the handwriting on the wall. They reaffirmed Moscow's belief that the Poles were unreliable as allies. Even worse, Solidarity had implications that reached beyond Poland; the Poles, after all, were notorious for saying and doing what those in the other satellites were merely thinking and wanted to do. These demonstrations showed that the Poles had learned how to organize themselves and to use modern international media. They revealed that this was not merely a problem of economics but one of security as well. After all, there was absolutely no difference in the political outlook of the average Polish worker and that of the average Polish soldier; they were, in the end, brothers. What implications did that have for the Warsaw Pact? Were the Polish (and, by implication, the Czech and Hungarian and even the East German) troops part of the Warsaw Pact, or were they, as Western diplomats liked to joke for years, special American parachute battalions already positioned behind the Soviet front lines?

Even in East Germany the changes finally took place. It was always the jewel in the crown, the single most important link in the postwar Soviet defense system, based on old and abiding (and quite justified) Soviet fears of an aggressive Germany. Broken off from its roots and completely subjugated, East Germany stood as the buffer between the West and the Soviet Union. East Germany as a nation was the wall before there was a wall. Once as a reporter in Warsaw I mentioned to a Polish friend the difficulty of Poland's political situation, lying, as it did, just to the west of Russia. "Oh, no," he answered, "it's much worse than that. We have Russia to the east of us, and Russia [referring to the twenty-one Russian divisions in East Germany] to the west of us."

But suddenly we see Honecker out of power and under house arrest, while outside wait a vast number of reporters and television teams. The televised stakeout is the ultimate humiliation, an East German version of Gary Hart. In Czechoslovakia, Dubçek, in political exile for twenty years in distant outposts of the bureaucracy, stands before a hundred thousand cheering Czechs, and Havel, recently out of jail, becomes president.

The last time I saw Prague was twenty-five years ago, when I was based in Warsaw. Czechoslovakia was part of my territory, and I had gone there for three weeks. The changes that finally resulted in the Prague Spring of 1968 were just beginning to take place; the Prague press was beginning to become freer, but in many ways Czechoslovakia was still the hardline country whose leadership had, some nine years earlier, sent troops to help subdue the Hungarian rebellion. In my brief three weeks in Prague I managed to displease the Party so much that I was called in to the Foreign Ministry. There a middle-level official repeated to me—it was no surprise—the names of everyone I had talked to in Prague. Then, in the voice of a tolerant older uncle, he told me that while I would not be expelled, I would not be welcome back in the country.

In the spring of 1990 I found myself back in the country at a meeting of American and Eastern European journalists. The Prague airport, which I had once found unusually oppressive with its excessive security procedures, is now open, and no visa is required. While in the past Czechs had grasped gratefully at the tiniest slivers of freedom, there is now the most exhilarating level of freedom of speech. At our conference a Russian journalist chastises the Americans present for failing to report more critically about Gorbachev. At lunch the next day the Czech president's press secretary, a man who in his previous incarnation was a translator of the most iconoclastic of America's writers, tells us under which conditions his government will jail reporters. It is not exactly a subject that thrills his audience, and the most violent cross-examination imaginable ensues; the lunch is arguably either a total disaster or possibly the greatest success of the week, as a workshop for the Eastern Europeans to see how passionately America's editors feel about freedom of the press.

If the freedoms are real, so are the old economic problems, which on certain days seem so severe as to be insurmountable. They make one think of how hard the path ahead is, how delicate the balance between political freedom and economic progress, and how we in America probably never understood this. As we have taken our freedoms for granted in much of this century, so we have taken the economic underpinnings of them for granted.

We spend the days talking about freedom and how to use it, and at night we talk about how hard the economics of it are. An American tells about Thomas Bata, the head of the Bata shoe company, who left Czechoslovakia after the Communists nationalized his factories. He went to Canada and remained extremely successful, the largest maker of shoes in the world. Now he has begun talking with the new government about manufacturing shoes in his homeland again. The questions are: Who owns the old factory now, and can Bata have it back? And beyond that, does he really want it back? The machinery is old, the skills of the workers there may be outdated, and the market is uncertain. He now has a modern factory in Malaysia with relatively low labor costs. If he chooses to reopen in Czechoslovakia, his best market may be to sell to the Soviet Union, and while Russia *looks like* a very big market, there is no guarantee that it will not turn out to be still the old Soviet Union—that is, a nonmarket in any profitable sense, which generates no valid currency in return.

As he speaks about Bata, my mind goes back twenty-five years, when, as an act of goodwill (this was before the major escalation in Vietnam and the resulting tensions), the U.S. Commerce Department sent a team of manufacturing experts to study Polish factories and make recommendations for improving them. I eagerly tagged along, for as a reporter I would not normally have been allowed inside the factories, and in addition, I would now be able to view them through the eyes of experts.

At dinner each night the Americans would talk about how primitive the factories were and how poorly the machinery was maintained. They were saddened by it; these were manufacturing men, and they instinctively hated the waste of manpower, material, and machinery and the inevitable poor quality of the final products that resulted. I asked the head of the delegation what chance the Poles had to compete in the world market. He explained to me how General Motors divided the market into different stalls and concluded that the Poles would not be able to make an entry at the Cadillac level or, for that matter, even the Buick, Olds, Pontiac, or Chevy level. Rather, their only hope was to make a low-level entry, in the (VW) Bug slot. As I remember those words, I realized that if this episode occurred today, it would probably be a Japanese team of experts and that the low end of the market would refer to the Koreans, Malaysians, and Taiwanese, but that in the new international economy, with the rise of East Asia, the entry-level spots would be the most, instead of the least, competitive.

For fifty years (and in some instances for centuries), the Eastern European nations were cut off from political freedoms and economic progress enjoyed in the West. The gap between their assumptions and hopes and those in the West are immense. A senior executive of *The New York Times* talks about the ratio between advertising and circulation revenues and notes that at the *Times* it is more than four to one; a Czech member of the panel points out that in his country there is no advertising because there is nothing to advertise. "We are a country," says one Eastern European panel member, "not of advertising but of antiadvertising."

Always in the crosscurrent of political debate in Poland and other Eastern European countries there is the scent of anti-Semitism. That few Jews are left in Poland and other parts of Eastern Europe matters little. (Of course, we can have anti-Semitism without Jews, notes a Polish friend; our country has traffic jams without cars.)

A Polish delegate tells of a recent forum at the University of Warsaw, where Adam Michnik, one of Solidarity's most talented young members, a man of exceptional skills and ability who has spent much of his adult life in jail, debates Jan Lopusynski, an ultranationalist member of Parliament. An audience question handed to Mr. Michnik addresses him as "Mr. Szechter." His mother was named Michnik; his father, Szechter, was connected to the old regime, as was a brother. In his youth, in order to separate himself from the odious regime, Adam took his mother's name, and Michnik has been his surname for his entire political career.

The question was a slap in the face. In Poland there are what are known as Polish names and Jewish names—and Szechter is a Jewish name. The question then is essentially anti-Semitic: It seeks to define the debate not in terms of the issues raised but in old and dark terms of Poles and Jews.

Mr. Michnik handled it extremely well: "Szechter is not my name. It is the name of my father. My name is Michnik. But if you mean by that question were my forefathers circumcised, the answer is yes."

What he was saying is: Judge me for my ideas; ideas are more important for the future of Poland than what you perceive as bloodlines. But it is hard to do so, particularly in times that are so difficult and when expectations fed by the modern media are so high.

It becomes clear that all kinds of tensions lie just beneath the surface here. As the week progresses, the delegates pay particular attention to the news from Poland, where the father of the new Eastern Europe political movements, Solidarity, seems about to fragment and where the government has already adapted a harsh, cold-shower method of trying to westernize the economy in the shortest possible time. Solidarity was unique in its capacity to unite the aspirations of an entire people. Opposition to the oppressors had provided unity, just as during the best days of the civil rights movement Jim Clark and Bull Connor helped Martin King unify a movement that might have splintered. When the victory finally came and the Communist government began to fall, a Polish friend of mine thought: The victory is finally ours; now the question is who are we. The potential for divisions was always there. Lech Wałesa, for all of his brilliance and courage, was always viewed by some of his colleagues as a man driven by emotion and instinct. One admirer said that he was not sophisticated enough to run a new free Poland, but had he been more sophisticated, he would have lacked the audacity to stand against the old regime.

Now inevitably Solidarity becomes more divided and thereby, involuntarily, more democratic. The Wałesa faction, with its roots in the Gdansk trade union movements—populist, blue-collar, rural—begins to pick up new allies, which are nationalistic and close to the Church (one of the main issues of such conservative and nationalistic groups becomes the desire to change Poland's liberal abortion laws, which had been fashioned by the Communists and which were always offensive to the Church). The other part of Solidarity, what one Pole calls the Warsaw-Cracow intellectual coalition, crystallizes around Prime

Minister Tadeusz Mazowiecki; it is urban, younger, better educated. Wałesa, says one pro-Wałesa newspaper in an attack on those who have moved over to Mazowiecki, does not have the smell of drawing-room perfume around him.

The division is painful for many Poles. "Like a divorce in the family," says Helen Luchzywo, one of the talented young journalists who has come to prominence as part of Solidarity, "like a divorce in a very young family." It is also hard on Wałesa; he was assisted by what was probably one of the ablest groups of advisers to help a political figure in this century. In the current split many, if not most of them, have gone over to the Mazowiecki faction; this has the effect of seeming to reduce Wałesa, making him appear frustrated. He would not be the first brilliant leader of a revolution—a role where good men live in a world of black and white—who found himself unsuited to the task of governing, filled as it is with gray decisions.

All over Eastern Europe there is now an immense variety of choices being offered under highly pressurized conditions, to peoples who have not made any choices of their own in half a century or more, and whose expectations have never been so high. The economic support system for such hopes is slight. The question is how long will it take for it to develop. "It will not happen in my or your lifetime," says my old friend Andrzej Wroblewski, a journalist who is now fifty-five, a man of honor who resigned from the weekly *Polityka* at the time of the imposition of martial law in 1982. "The gap is great. The question is how well, how democratically, we will use that time in which we try to catch up. Do we use it to scapegoat others—do we feel sorry for ourselves and blame our conditions on the Communists and the Jews—or do we accept responsibility for it ourselves, that whatever brought us to this point was beyond the control of almost anyone in the country, and accept the fact that it will take a great deal of very hard work to catch up? It does not help us to make accusations; we must understand that in the West things work because people work hard and accept responsibility for their lives. We can drive the last few Communists out of the government; they are almost gone anyway, and that will make us feel good for at least a day when the last handful are gone. The temptation to make accusations against others, to find fault with someone else rather than ourselves and to blame our conditions on others, that is almost overwhelming, particularly as we find out how hard it is to catch up."

Wroblewski tells a story about a young man who shows up at a Warsaw circus and offers to jump every night from the highest wire to the ground without a net. He charges ten dollars for this act. The manager is intrigued but demands a trial jump before he signs him on. Up goes the young would-be acrobat and does his death-defying number. His landing is hard, but he picks himself up and walks shakily over to the manager. "Let's make it fifteen dollars a night," he says. "Why the sudden increase in price?" asks the manager. "I had no idea it was going to hurt so much," the acrobat says.

However, I think it would be a mistake to underestimate in the long run the energy that is going to be released as the nations of Eastern Europe are freed from the doctrinaire economic and political systems that have burdened them for so long. Granted, the industrial infrastructure is weak and at best badly atrophied; granted, the currencies too are weak and expectations surely exceed possibilities for the moment. The great question before the four main Eastern European countries (East Germany, Poland, Czechoslovakia, and Hungary) is how much of their social coherence and political unity came directly from their enduring opposition to those who would govern them and how much now remains. The work ethic within those countries has always been powerful; Central Europe was an important source in providing many of the best workers in America earlier in this century, when our own core economy was in its prime. The modern educational systems of these countries are a great deal better than most foreigners realize; the great sadness was that their educated people had nothing left to do after they graduated. That, as much as anything else, was the source of the deep and abiding criticism one found there. Though their educational systems were highly politicized, an observer always had a sense that both teachers and students had a deft ability to separate that which was real education from that which was educational agitprop. It may be the ironic legacy that the only thing the Communists bequeathed to their people was an improved educational standard.

The political opening up of these societies, with the passionate desire of so many for greater freedom, may well be more difficult and complicated than anyone realizes. There has been an assumption that great economic progress will automatically follow political independence. The problem for the new governments will be balancing harsh realities against unrealistic expectations. There is no sure model for any of them, nor is there historical tradition to draw on. David Broder, writing in *The Washington Post,* quoted one Polish journalist as saying that the prospect of bringing a new definition of freedom to Poland was like a drunken surgeon performing an operation he had never done before. No, said a colleague, "it is like a sober surgeon operating on an animal he's never seen before." But the economic transformation, with even the smallest approximation of a second Marshall Plan on the part of West Germany, Japan, and others, is likely to surprise us. The people of this vast region have been compelled by forces outside their control to live for some forty years far beneath the standard of living achieved first in America, then in Western Europe, and finally in Japan. John Chancellor, the distinguished television commentator, told me that his most striking memory of covering those euphoric days in Berlin when the wall came down was "the look on the faces of the East Berliners when they got to Ka De We, the Bloomingdale's of West Berlin. I had thought," he added, "that they would be dazzled by the luxury goods. Instead, they were enraged; you could see it on their faces. They'd been held prisoner in East Berlin all those years while people just a mile away were living the good life. They weren't mad at the West Berliners; they were furious with their jailers in the East." Then Chancellor added—this was November 23, 1989—"I don't think Herr Krenz is going to last very long." He lasted six weeks.

That sense of a better life finally coming within reach is going to be a powerful force. I think that for all the immense economic problems ahead it will manifest itself sooner than we think. The people in Eastern Europe will be driven by the same hunger that drives contemporary Asia. That energy will enhance not merely the Eastern European countries themselves but also *Europe* as a continent and an idea.

In America there have been those who write of the recent events in Eastern Europe as if they were victories of the American way or for capitalism. Victories they are, for those who have endured the terrible suffering of those ugly regimes and for those who helped bring about the changes and now have a chance for a better life. Victories for *our* side they are not. They do present opportunities.

After all, this is something for which we have hungered for forty years. Ironically, now as the opportunities finally open up, we are ill prepared to exploit them. Our response to the Poles, Czechs, Hungarians, and others as they ask for help, for a new Marshall Plan, is minimal. In another age we probably would have paid what they asked through the CIA just to stage a coup; now that the old regimes are collapsing, we must be involuntarily tightfisted.

If there is one nation likely to be the main beneficiary of this change, to fill the vacuum created by the departure of the Soviet Union, it is Germany. I, like others, sense that Germany, with its discipline, its economic energy, its seeming economic priorities, will catapult to a new level of dynamism and strength. One of the limits on West Germany in the past was the size of its market. That is going to change. Another limit has been that imposed by its birthrate, in particular its lack of young people. That, too, is going to change with the new connection to East Germany. West Germany's economic relationship with the countries of Eastern Europe is historic. There is magnetic force there with a power of its own; for more than twenty-five years the West Germans have been seeding the territory economically and culturally. The younger generation of Eastern Europeans might above all else admire things American—sweaters, jeans, American rock music, and *Playboy* magazine—but it is the Germans who have been sending economic missions, lending money, and publishing Polish, Czech, and Hungarian writers in Germany. The Germans have been getting ready for this moment for a long time.

They are the engine that has driven much of the economy of Western Europe in recent years. A British financier, asked if there is fear of the growing power of West Germany, particularly now at the time of the vacuum created by the Soviets, seems surprised by the question. Fear? he said, pondering the question. No, rather an awareness of how much we all need them.

Some are making comparisons between the Germans and the Japanese. Like the Japanese, German culture is economically oriented, and it is even more oriented toward manufacturing exports. German financial markets are strong, disciplined, and connected to reality. Their per capita GNP by some surveys is second only to that of the United States and has been ascending as ours has flattened out. But if the Japanese are the electronic tribe, then the Germans are the smokestack tribe. Their leaders do not talk (as the Japanese have) of leading the way into the twenty-first century; indeed, they seem perfectly content with the twentieth century. Their companies do not pour money into research and development (R&D). Pure science matters less there than here or in Japan or, for that matter, in France. They do not rush to discover the next generation of computers.

Instead, their great strength is that they do things the old-fashioned way, and they do them well. Being an engineer is a significantly higher calling there than it is in the United States. Those who make things derive from it not merely pleasure, but a kind of societal respect missing here. They disdain the quality of foreign workmanship: Mercedes, for example, will not manufacture outside the country because it believes it cannot get the requisite quality of worker. Germany is still a country where craftsmanship is so important that young people will invest several years in apprenticeships. But the Germans have adapted well to the modern economy; they have used what they call defusion energy to modernize—that is, to bring the uses of chips and computers into the traditional workplace. They have systematically updated their traditional industrial infrastructure. They seem strong and competent, like America in the fifties and early sixties.

They put their energy into doing what they have always done, trying to do it just a little bit better each year. They do not depend on business schools; heads of their companies tend to be engineers or economists who are loyal to their products, to their workers, and to their communities. The expectations of the company owners and managers are realistic, often modest compared with ours. They worry about market share and quality of product. Relationships with esteemed customers are taken very seriously. There is not much talk about fast tracks. Nor are German managers likely to call up consulting companies and demand that they send over two or three young men fresh out of business school to tell them how to run their companies. Some might call Germany and its economy old-fashioned and stolid, but they would have to admit it is strong.

III

THE INTERESTING THING ABOUT THE Soviet brand of communism was that it never worked. A visitor to Russia and to Eastern Europe soon found out that the Soviets had invented the first two-tiered economic system. There was the official system, as promulgated by the government, and then there was the real economy, which was the black market. The two economies had nothing to do with each other, and nothing got done without use of the black market.

Yet almost by instinct, perhaps because we built up a dynamic that depended on the Soviet threat for its very existence, we always magnified the threat. Unlike great power struggles in the past (in which one side had access to oil, and the other did not), neither power really sought anything held by the other. If anything, it was a case of two essentially isolationist nations catapulted too quickly to superpower status, each burdened by fear and insecurity in a new atomic age. (Two blind dinosaurs struggling in a pit, each thinking the other the aggressor, I always thought. Years later I read of J. Robert Oppenheimer's description: two scorpions in a jar, each able to give a nuclear sting to the other, but only at the price of its own death.)

For men and women of my generation the Cold War was the dominant fact of life. One could not have imagined an American political debate without the issue of standing up to the Soviet Union as its centerpiece; in its most recent incarnation Ronald Reagan came to power because Jimmy Carter was perceived as being too soft on communism, and Carter himself was greatly aided in his quest for the presidency because Gerald Ford seemed to think Poland in 1976 was outside the reach of Soviet power.

I was twelve in 1946 when Winston Churchill gave his Iron Curtain speech in Fulton, Missouri, in effect the official notification that we lived in a divided world. A year later George Marshall announced the Marshall Plan for European recovery; in 1948 the Czech coup took place. I was sixteen when the Korean War began and Joseph McCarthy gave his maiden anti-Communist speech. Later, when I attended Harvard, the place was dominated by the challenge of the Cold War, despite claims made by McCarthy and others that it was a center of left-wing activity. In fact, most of the young faculty in political science were hardheaded and eager for the challenge ahead. The struggle with the Soviets dominated Harvard's Government (political science) department, which in the immediate postwar years was the hot, new department on campus, the place where reputations were made and connections forged. Three of Harvard's young instructors from that period went on to be chief national security advisers to Presidents of the United States—Bundy, Kissinger, and Brzezinski—and a fourth, James Schlesinger, who was in the economics department, served as both secretary of defense and director of the CIA.

I was nineteen in 1953, when Stalin died, and barely out of college when the Soviet tanks rode into Budapest and crushed the Hungarian Revolution. In 1961 as a foreign correspondent I listened to the wireless in Katanga as the news of the construction of the Wall came over the nightly BBC broadcast, adding the permanence of mortar and brick to the ideological divisions of those years. Later that year I listened in Saigon to the news of the Cuban missile crisis. It was the ultimate moment of terror, as the two superpowers came to terms with their roles. In the end we lived in a numbed acceptance of it all. Now, as the Cold War winds down, we still hear the echoes. A former secretary of defense meeting with friends at the Century Club says in his gravest tone that now is the most dangerous time of all, when the Soviet Union is being peaceful. In the Soviet Union, likewise, hard-line critics of Gorbachev are critical of his quick pullback from Eastern Europe. Eduard Shevardnadze, the Soviet foreign minister, retaliated by calling them McCarthyites. He says they are really asking, "Who lost Eastern Europe?" and suggesting, "Why did we not use tanks for the restoration of order?" Then he adds: "Is it possible that we have learned nothing. Have we forgotten the lessons of Afghanistan? Have we forgotten 1956 and 1968?" Socialism and the friendship of true neighbors, he adds, cannot be based "on bayonets, tanks, or blood."

Because of geography, each nation had been historically isolationist; in both cases, internationalism was acquired involuntarily. The Soviets became a great power because the war ended with the mighty Red Army placed in the heart of Europe; that which others saw as an empire they saw as a buffer designed against invasion from the West. We became a world power by being pulled, against our will, into two European wars within some twenty years, and we had to fill a role left vacant by an exhausted England. There probably would have been tension between the U.S.A. and USSR under the best of circumstances, but the sheer horror of Joseph Stalin's rule, plus the coming of nuclear and thermonuclear weapons, exaggerated the tension.

Internationalist we might have become, but our prewar isolationist sentiments were still powerful. As Communism unraveled in Eastern Europe, I was at work on a book on the 1950's. It was like living in a time warp. As I watched the mounting euphoria of that nine-month period in 1989 and 1990, I was also reliving a nine-month period that took place during Harry Truman's presidency in late 1949 and early 1950. Equally startling events were taking place then: In September 1949 came the news that the Soviets had successfully detonated an atomic bomb, ending the American atomic monopoly upon which our entire defense strategy was based. Next came the final collapse of Chiang on mainland China, then the conviction of Alger Hiss and the news that Klaus Fuchs, a top British atomic scientist, had confessed to spying for the Communists. In late January 1950 Truman decided (over the objections of almost all his scientific experts) to go ahead with a new bomb called the Super or Hydrogen bomb. The domestic anxiety caused by these events helped result in Joseph McCarthy's assaults, starting in February 1950. McCarthyism in general turned out to be strong in parts of the country where antiwar feeling had been strong before World War II and where, on occasion, the people believed that if we had had to go to war, we had chosen the wrong enemy.

Our internationalism actually contained a good measure of anticommunism—that is, internationalism sold in the name of anticommunism. Inevitably there was what Toynbee calls historical transference—we took on some of the coloration of their society. As they were secretive, we ourselves became more secretive; as Stalin was the most paranoid of figures, some of that paranoia inevitably took root here. My favorite statement of the symbiotic dynamic of the Cold War comes from the movie of *The Spy Who Came In from the Cold.* Control, the British top agent (who bears a striking physical resemblance to Richard

Helms, then the head of the CIA) is ruminating aloud on the ethics of his trade: "Our work, as I understand it, is based on a single assumption that we are never going to be the aggressor. We do disagreeable things, but we *are* defensive. Our policies are peaceful, but we can't afford to be less ruthless than those of the opposition. . . . Can we? . . . ." Control pauses, then continues, "No, I'd say that since the war, our methods, our techniques, that is, and those of the Communists have been very much the same. . . . Yes, I mean occasionally we've had to do wicked things indeed, but you can't be less wicked than your enemies simply because your government's policy is benevolent."

Intelligent, analytical men in our national security apparatus looked at any other nation in the world and quickly and accurately assessed both its strengths and weaknesses. Yet they looked at the Soviet Union and found strengths it demonstrably lacked and ambitions it did not manifest. A hard look at the Soviet Union would have revealed weaknesses everywhere: in its agriculture; in its industrial production; in the quality of its goods; in its housing; even in its capacity to motivate ordinary citizens to do ordinary tasks. In technology the gap widened dramatically throughout the period.

The effect of nuclear weapons on American political debate was formidable. It allowed isolationists to pose as internationalists; it was a weapon that promised to solve all problems yet could not be used. It dramatically increased the anxiety of ordinary people and almost surely moved all political and military debate significantly to the right. Those who favored its use were on the far right in most debates, and even if they did not prevail, they nonetheless managed to make those who opted for other, more moderate military solutions appear to be more centrist. One has only to consider J. Robert Oppenheimer. He is regarded by many as the first great dove of the post–World

War II era and perhaps the most important early victim of the Cold War. Certainly he abhorred the decision to build the hydrogen bomb and he tried to prevent it, both overtly and covertly. But when he was forced to come up with some alternative to the Super, he seized on tactical nuclear weapons—not exactly the most dovish of options. The very lack of choices reflected how far the Super had shifted the center of the debate.

The truth was that the possession of the bomb was for both superpowers oddly paralyzing. Edward Teller, considered by many the father of the hydrogen bomb, liked to tell a story of a lunch he had with Oppenheimer and I. I. Rabi in November 1952, when the Korean War was stalemated. Oppenheimer turned to Teller and said, "Well, Edward, now that you have your H-bomb, why don't you use it to end the war in Korea?" Teller answered: "The use of weapons is none of my business. This is a political decision, and I will have no part of it." It was that kind of era.

From the start the engine behind developing the hydrogen bomb was the politics of the Cold War rather than any real military need. The Joint Chiefs, other than the Air Force Chief of Staff, were at least partially ambivalent. General Omar Bradley testified that the only military advantage of the H-bomb was psychological. Such early dissenters as Oppenheimer and Conant of Harvard argued that a thermonuclear weapon did not add security but indeed diminished it by placing so vast an investment in a weapons strategy that could not be used. But the policy makers were not interested in such arguments; if there was the chance for the creation of a superweapon, no matter how terrible and how unusable, no politician—particularly a President already being blamed for losing some six hundred million Chinese to communism—dared face his voters and say that he or she had not pursued it.

It is possible that future historians will sum up the forty-year struggle with the Soviets not harshly but in fact quite gently. They may see it not in terms of marvelous opportunities squandered or of unseemly national arrogance manifested by both sides but perhaps as an inevitable stage in the growth of two new essentially isolationist superpowers (each possessing arms unprecedented in terms of destructiveness). I suspect historians will concentrate on something altogether different in this period: the rise of nonwhite nations first to political independence and then somewhat more slowly and erratically to genuine economic independence. In that history the opening event will be World War II, which significantly weakened the dominating colonial powers throughout the world. Japan's military strike throughout East Asia was the beginning of the end for the mystique of the white man's power, and it accelerated the demand for independence. The watershed was Dien Bien Phu in 1954, and other dates of significance are the American decision to halt the French-British-Israeli strike against Nasser, the defeat of the French in Algiers, the Bay of Pigs, the American failure in Vietnam and departure from Saigon, the attempts of the Arab nations to gain some measure of political control over the price of oil, the expulsion of various Russian delegations from such Arab and African nations as Egypt and Guinea, the Russian defeat in Afghanistan, and finally—for the economic component is as important as the political one—the economic rise first of Japan and then of the Little Tigers in Asia. (Never having been colonized and always having had many of the characteristics of the industrial powers, Japan never really qualified as an underdeveloped nation.)

If there is an irony to all this, it is that much of this struggle, colonized against colonizer, nonwhite against white, was seen, particularly in the West, not within its proper context, as being primarily anticolonial or antineocolonial, but rather as an extension of the Cold War. Caught as we were in that greater dynamic of anticommunism, we could not see our adversaries as nationalists. We had to see them as Communists and thus as enemies. The additional irony, since almost all these nations were breaking away from Western countries, was that their ally was the Soviet Union. This most stagnant and static of societies, by almost any standard the least revolutionary of the major powers, was perceived, however inaccurately, as a broker of and sympathizer to revolution. Thus the successes of indigenous people were seen in the minds of Western policy makers as part of a giant game plan designed in Moscow.

Because its former colonies were breaking away, the West was portrayed as being in decline, which was not true; what was in decline was the West as a sponsor and beneficiary of a colonial era. In fact, the Western nations were far healthier than anyone realized. It is intriguing to ponder how different the last forty years might have been for America if, first, it had seen the Communist challenge not as an apocalyptic event, part theological, part political, but rather as a crude and often incompetent manifestation of traditional Russian nationalism; second, if we had had a better sense of the limits of our power, particularly in Asia, where Douglas MacArthur was so vainglorious and egomaniacal that he refused to recognize signs the Chinese were sending him in the fall of 1950 (that they had, in fact, crossed the Yalu and would enter the war if we pushed too close to it), thereby escalating a war that was winding down; and if, third, the architects of the Vietnam War had heeded General Ridgway's 1954 warning on the dangers of being impaled there.

Probably the first sign that the Soviet threat had diminished and that there was a de facto stalemate that negated not merely atomic weapons but significant use of land armies as well came in 1966, when De Gaulle took France out of NATO. Within the West there was a great deal of uneasiness and criticism about Gallic selfishness, ego, and disloyalty.

But there was nothing we could do to stop him. At the time there was a good deal of talk that this reflected poorly on the Western alliance and that it was a reflection of the weakness of the West, particularly the United States. The Soviet Union did not have this kind of problem with *its* allies; therefore, it was presumed to be better at realpolitik. Yet, if anything, De Gaulle's move was a sign of the true strength of the West, that despite the high force levels, massive military spending, and threatening rhetoric of the United States and USSR, France no longer needed NATO and wanted a more independent policy, albeit within essentially the same orbit as the West. In retrospect the French withdrawal marked the signal victory of American postwar policy in Europe. Those who were to be contained had been contained.

The dynamic of the Cold War became ever more damaging to those two nations most caught up in it. They were forced to pay an ever-higher price at the expense of their own economic health; even when it was clear that the policy of containment in Europe had worked, we extended it to parts of the world where for historical and cultural reasons it was hardly appropriate. In the eighties both countries went on a binge of buying and building weapons that implied that containment had never worked in the first place. Most American critics, trying to judge the damage of those years, look at the enormity of Defense Department spending as the crux of the problem. I see it as only the tip of the iceberg. The real damage was in the corruption of political dialogue—of the confusion between what was real and what had been mandated as real.

As the Cold War was ending, those immune to it, or skilled at paying lip service and getting on with their own agenda, like the Japanese, prospered. The new century was not about a great power struggle between America and the Soviet Union.

* * *

The American Century, as Naohiro Amaya, the Japanese economic and political theorist, has pointed out was really an Oil Century or an Oil Culture. Henry Ford invented the Model T and prospectors hit their great strikes in the American Southwest at almost the same time. Thus the basic ingredients suddenly came together. Ford not only created a car that could be mass-produced but kept bringing down the price so that the workers could become the consumers as well. We led the world in mechanization and thus democratized our society at the same time; through oil we brought middle-class status to a mass society.

World War II gave us the political, social, and diplomatic confidence to act upon our abundant industrial might. At that time only three nations seemed not to know how powerful the United States really was: Japan, Germany, and America. Of America's decision to enter the war, Churchill noted: "Hitler's fate was sealed. Mussolini's fate was sealed. As for the Japanese, they would be ground to powder. All the rest was merely the proper application of overwhelming force."

As good a date as any to mark the true coming of the American Century is the Battle of Midway from June 4 to June 6, 1942. We had been unprepared at the outbreak of the war, our Navy devastated in the surprise attack at Pearl Harbor. Yet only seven months later, at Midway, our industrial capacity and our sources of natural energy were so great that we inflicted on the Japanese what was probably the crucial defeat of the war. At Midway, using land- and carrier-based planes, we sank four Japanese carriers and one heavy cruiser, while losing one destroyer and one aircraft carrier. Even had Admiral Chester Nimitz lost more carriers at Midway, as Paul Kennedy points out, his losses would have been quickly replaced by three new fleet carriers, three light fleet carriers, and fifteen escort carriers, and in 1943 by *five* fleet carriers, six light carriers, and twenty-five escort carriers. With our great assembly lines and our ever-expanding industrial core (and protected as we were by two great oceans in an age when weaponry could not yet cross an ocean), we became the industrial arsenal for the mightiest of war efforts. In 1942 and 1943 America alone produced almost twice as many airplanes as the entire Axis. In 1943 and 1944 we were producing one ship a day and an airplane every five minutes.

It was an Oil War in the Oil Century, but only the Allies had complete and easy access to oil. As Clarence "Bud" Anderson, one of the great aces of World War II, wrote in his new book, *To Fly and Fight,* of the period in 1944 when the skies increasingly belonged to the Allies: "For the past several weeks, the Eighth Air Force had been targeting oil and Ludwigshafen-Mannheim was a center for synthetic fuels. Oil was everything, the lifeblood of war. Nations can't fight without oil. All through my training and all through the war I can't remember ever being limited on how much I could fly. There was always fuel enough. But by 1944 the Germans weren't so fortunate. They were feeling the pinch from the daily bombardments. Without fuel and lubricants their war machine would eventually grind to a stop. Now that the Mustang fighters were arriving in numbers, capable of escorting the bombers all the way to their targets and back, Germany's oil industry was there for the pounding. The day would come, and it would be soon, when the German Air Force, the Luftwaffe, would begin picking its spots, contesting some missions, and not others; or concentrating on isolated bomber formations, to the exclusion of all the rest, largely at random from what we could tell. The Luftwaffe's idea was to conserve fuel and pilots. . . ." For Americans of that generation, two images summed up the war, both of them from *Life* magazine. The first was the familiar image of the battlefield dead of both sides, captured with a remarkable new realism by better, smaller, and faster cameras; the second was American factories pouring out jeeps, tanks, and planes— American military industrial products lined up as far as the eye can see.

We finished one of the darkest periods in human history more optimistic than ever. Our gross national product was greater than at the beginning of the war. As Kennedy points out, in 1939, using 1939 dollars, our GNP was $88.6 billion, and in 1945 it was $135 billion. When World War II was over, we were rich and confident in a world that was poor and pessimistic. Those who had been powerful before the war were devastated, some in victory, some in defeat. England, a victor, bled white in World War I, exhausted by World War II, was physically and economically depleted and about to cut loose its colonies. France was also a victor, but a victor humiliated by the dismal showing of its armies early in the war and the collaboration of so many of its citizens with the Germans. It was also preparing to fight two costly colonial wars, ironically to regain its lost honor as much as anything else. Germany was entirely destroyed, with millions dead. Its land was physically divided by its conquerors (its means of production and its market thereby effectively cut in half). The Soviet Union was also a victor, but it had lost twenty-six million people. It was as ravaged in victory as Germany was in defeat, and it was governed by one of the most brutal tyrants of the century. As for Japan, not only had it been defeated and ravaged physically, but spiritually—a certain vision of Japanese greatness had died as well.

We saw it as our proper due that the war had made us stronger. We saw ourselves as more modern than Europe; with no feudal tradition, we were the new modern classless society cut loose from the social and political shackles of the past. This moment would be, we assumed, not merely a brief historical accident, but rather a permanent condition. At home an abundance of human energy was being unleashed. We had easy access to cheap oil, first at home and then later, as we began to hit domestic limitations, from our secondary sources in the Middle East, where we could still determine the price. The Depression was over, but the New Deal legislation that was designed to end it had helped democratize the postwar workplace. If the first Henry Ford had turned bitterly against the implications of his own deeds and become the most virulent antilabor figure in the country, then right in Detroit was the proof that the country had changed, that a new, more humane generation of American business leaders was taking over. There his grandson, Henry Ford II, spoke out for a new industrial democracy and for the rights of ordinary workers.

The GI Bill democratized the educational process as the New Deal had democratized the workplace. A generation of young Americans who might have had no choice but to stay in small towns and inherit the modest jobs held by their fathers had gone out into the world because of the war and had discovered previously undreamed-of possibilities. They left behind any notions about their limited ability to define their roles in life, and more often than not, aided by the GI Bill, they were the first members of their families to go to college and thus to break out of class alignments. The result was a staggering increase in social fluidity. It was a double release of energy, for not only were the children of the new meritocracy hungry, but they forced the children of the old aristocracy, who might in another day have coasted, to work harder as well.

America seemed to be heading for a future that would set it apart from the Old World. In Europe, no matter what your skills and intelligence, you were a prisoner of the past, likely to be what your parents and grandparents had been, a member of the same class, and no better educated. In America, by contrast, the past meant nothing. Here you could reinvent yourself and be whoever you wanted to be. The children of immigrants who had lived in tenements and who had never owned anything were going to college and moving to the suburbs, where they were buying houses.

There was a belief in America that the war had been fought not so much for realpolitik as for moral and democratic reasons. This new egalitarian spirit—and the technological and intellectual needs of America as a new superpower—mandated that the governing class would no longer come exclusively from the old elite. Therefore, the schools of the old elite had to be democratized. I was told as a freshman that my class at Harvard, which entered in the fall of 1951, was the first that contained more public school graduates than prep school graduates. As I remember it, the prep school graduates were far better prepared, had better reading and writing skills, and excelled for the first two years. But, by the end of the sophomore year, the public high school graduates had learned how to study and, perhaps because they were hungrier, they surged ahead—in turn causing the preppies to work harder.

By the mid-fifties ordinary people had a sense that their lives were going to be better than those of their parents. If anything defined the period, it was a new sense of optimism that the future was going to be better than the past. Leaders from Europe who came here were impressed by the confidence that existed among all Americans, the abundant belief that this was America's moment. Japanese who came over here to study our industrial success saw America as the most wondrous and open of modern societies, where they felt free from the class distinctions that existed at home. They were not so much impressed by the finished products of our great factories, or by the informality of the men who ran them (here subordinates called bosses by their first names), or by the openness of the Americans

62

toward the Japanese themselves, who had so recently been a sworn enemy. Rather, they were astonished by the homes of ordinary blue-collar workers. These were not tiny apartments but houses, equipped with what seemed like fully automatic kitchens, and downstairs were dens where there might be pool tables. Even more miraculous, the workers *owned* the houses. This was a nation living a dream, a dream shared with increasing numbers of its citizens.

There was by the 1960's a distant rumble of political protest on the campuses, but ironically, it was taking place among the children of the upper middle class, the children of affluence. It was a protest not against personal hardship or tyranny but against the values inherent in a culture of affluence and bigness.

The high-water mark of it all, I think, was 1964. It came some twenty years after the end of World War II, so that not only had the economy been expanding for 20 years, but the strength of the economy was now manifest in the confidence of the political system. Lyndon Johnson was planning the Great Society, the final step in bringing the American Dream to every household. That year the Ford Motor Company brought out the Mustang, a sporty, sexy car produced primarily for what was deemed the youth market. Johnson had opened his election campaign in Detroit on Labor Day with Henry Ford II on one side of him and Walter Reuther on the other. Clearly he was the candidate of the new, classless America.

But Johnson's assault on class barriers implicit in the Great Society turned out to be less successful than we hoped at the time. For one thing, to the degree that America was a success, it was primarily monoracial; we had only just begun to move toward full political and legal citizenship for our black population. We had no idea how difficult the economic and educational components of that goal would prove. Much of the nation's black population remained invisible to the eyes of white policy makers; much of it was still in the South, suffering from crushing agrarian poverty and just beginning to move north in hopes of finding a better life in the great industrial cities (just as the number of blue-collar jobs was beginning to decline). Mostly this black population had been deliberately denied adequate education for more than a century. The dramatic changes in the law and the mass migration were only beginning to reveal how serious our racial problem was. Even the most benign court rulings touched only the legal aspects of the dilemma. We were, almost without knowing it, simply transforming a black illiterate agrarian population into a black urban underclass.

If ever an event marked the outer limit of American power, though, it was Vietnam. As individuals we may have come to terms with what went wrong, but we never have as a nation. The most articulate architects of it, who talk privately about what went wrong, have yet to say publicly they made a mistake; Richard Nixon, who was in no small measure elected in 1968 because of the wrenching divisions Vietnam created within the Democratic party, went on to call it our finest hour. As such, Vietnam remains out there like a meal that has never been finished—and never taken off the table either.

In June 1950, when America still had not felt its super-affluence, Harry Truman instinctively committed troops to Korea, but he hated doing so. He feared what it would do to his small defense budget. In 1954, when Ike pondered whether to send bombers and troops to rescue the French troops at Dien Bien Phu, General Ridgway, acting on his own, sent a study team to find out the actual logistics of intervening in Vietnam. He concluded that air power would not bring about a French victory; it would only involve America even more deeply. The military needs for ground troops would be huge, Ridgway believed—at least five and possibly ten divisions (between fifty thousand and one million men)—and because of the primitive conditions that would favor the indigenous troops, it would require fifty-five engineering battalions. Draft calls would be higher than Korea, perhaps a hundred thousand a month, and unlike the Korean War, this war would be fought with a hostile population lurking in the background. Ike saw the report, realized as a professional soldier how exhausting the war would be and how destructive it would be to his budget. So the idea of intervention died despite the grandiosity of John Foster Dulles's rhetoric. This was a nation still in touch with its limits, a democracy, not yet an empire.

A decade later, after ten years of unparalleled affluence, those restraints were gone. No one worried about costs anymore. There was no one in the government to play the role of Ridgway, to force the architects of the war to see the full costs of any such adventure. We were a nation that could have it all. Thus, when it became clear in the fall of 1965 that a small commitment of perhaps only twenty thousand men was not going to work, that the North Vietnamese Army was coming into the country faster than we were, Johnson and McNamara geared up for a big war of five hundred thousand men or quite possibly more.

Johnson wanted more than anything else to push the Great Society through Congress. He was sure that the Congress would, if given a choice, choose the war over the Great Society, so he and McNamara, the war's principal architect, deliberately decided to lie about the size of the war and not to go, despite the anguished pleas of his economists, for the rather small tax increase needed to pay for it. It was a moment of supreme arrogance. We were so rich we could have not merely guns and butter but tricky bookkeeping as well. They were, as Ed Dale, a *Times* economic reporter, noted at the time, "running the war on the margin." So not only did we enter an unwinnable war, but by lying to ourselves, we started running a deficit that began a crushing inflation, which helped emphasize rather than eradicate class lines in America.

Certainly the Vietnam War expedited the end of the American Century. If the American Century was an Oil Century, then World War II had been the perfect Oil Century war, for both sides were fully mechanized, and, fortunately for the Allies, we had almost all the oil. World War II gave our policy makers an illusion of American military power in Asia that subsequent Pacific wars did not bear out, since our adversaries, unlike the Japanese, were not Oil Century military powers. In Korea our technological ability was both an advantage and a disadvantage. We expected too much of our mechanization, and for a time we were prisoners of our own machinery: Our troops stayed too close to the roads (more often than not in the valleys) and were vulnerable to the night strikes of the Chinese, whose vast army moved virtually without oil and who, especially in the early going, went where there were no roads, to the high ground. Vietnam, even more so than Korea, showed how seriously the belief in our vastly superior technology could mislead our policy makers. Here we were heliborne, and we brought the ultimate mechanized force to fight a jungle war against an enemy that was among the least mechanized forces of the modern era. At one point in 1965, during arguments over whether or not to intervene, Curtis LeMay, the famed Air Force general of World War II, the architect of the highly successful low-level bombing of Tokyo, talked about the need to bomb the other side into the Stone Age. What if they're already there? asked McGeorge Bundy in a prophetic moment.

Vietnam made us understand in some terrible way that we were no longer a mere democracy; we were a superpower, a democracy become empire. A democracy functions on the basis of shared truths, but an empire is far grander, it is about power, and truth often becomes an obstruction. Ironically enough, warnings about the danger of going from a democracy to an empire had been issued by Robert A. Taft during the early forties as he argued against America's entering what he considered a European war. One of the leading isolationists in the U.S. Senate, he was completely unable to adapt his politics to the rise of modern global totalitarian states, but he was oddly prophetic about the price America would pay for its victory in the War. In direct contradiction to Henry Luce's theory of an American Century, he argued that if we won, there would be a new age of Anglo-American imperialism, for which we were not suited by our democratic instinct and ideals. He saw Luce as the would-be policeman of the world and America in the twentieth century playing the role England had in the nineteenth. The American Century, Taft said in the spring of 1943, "is based on the theory that we know better what is good for the world than the world itself. It assumes that we are always right and that everyone who disagrees with us is wrong."

The Vietnam War was a large part of my life, and much of what I believe in (and no longer believe in) was forged there. I was in those days part of a small group of pessimistic correspondents who were much criticized for being too liberal, too cowardly, and too young. There was a systematic assault upon our careers and reputations, and it was orchestrated by the White House, the Pentagon, and their proxies in Saigon. If we were guilty of anything in those days, it was not of being too liberal, a word that did not apply to Vietnam, or too cowardly (most of us saw more combat than our journalist colleagues in World War II did), but of being too rational, of being too serious, of taking too seriously our attempts to achieve journalistic truth.

We did not realize that America had become an empire, run by men suited to running empires, men who did not necessarily value the truth. They were far too grand for that; they valued power over truth. They had created their own truth: In power there was truth. We journalists, too innocent for our own good, still believed in the power of truth, believed that if only they, the good people of Washington, knew what we knew, if we could get over the heads of their somewhat dim-witted military proxies in Saigon, we might change the perceptions of those giving the marching orders.

One episode remains remarkably clear some twenty-seven years after the fact, though at the time I did not appreciate its true meaning. It was the early fall of 1963, and McNamara was on one of his many flying visits to Vietnam. Henry Cabot Lodge was the new American ambassador, and unlike his predecessors, he thought the reporting from Saigon very good and the war itself in bad shape. He asked a group of us to brief McNamara privately. We debated the wisdom of doing this, for it is not the job of reporters to hold private briefings for high public officials, but in the end we agreed because Lodge had been helpful to us and was extremely persuasive. There had been a great deal of misunderstanding of our reporting in the Pentagon, he argued, and at the very least this would allow the secretary to see that we were good, patriotic, and even tough-minded citizens.

That day, as we filed into the meeting room—there were, I think, five of us—we were suddenly instructed that there were new ground rules for the briefing. We could talk to the secretary about the *political* situation in Vietnam but not the *military* situation. I was stunned. Our military sources, including the now-legendary John Paul Vann, were brilliant, the best in the country. They had tutored us well for more than a year, and we were wired to them. We had been primed to tell McNamara that the war had never been fought by our proxies and that far from being virtually won, as his generals were claiming, it was virtually lost. In retrospect I wish I had walked out then and there. At the time I did not understand the shrewdness of what

McNamara had done. It was the typical act of a man who was one of the most skillful bureaucratic infighters and dissemblers of his time. He had understood immediately how important it was not to hear the truth. If he could set such ground rules, he could go back and say in good conscience (for he was always a man of good conscience) that everything he had heard about the military situation was relatively positive. He knew the rules of the empire far better than we did.

In the end we both were naive, he about Vietnam, and we journalists about Washington. In the ensuing years, thanks in no small part to meetings like this, both of us became a great deal less naive. That is but one example of how the Cold War crushed truth, how the need for power overwhelmed the need for truth.

America was, in the words of the German writer Günther Grass, twice punished by Vietnam—first, because we had done it and, second, because we never came to terms with what we had done. At best we left Vietnam involuntarily tempered by battlefield defeat. However, we did not temper our rhetoric; we boasted, if not to the world, at least to ourselves, of what we could still do and pledged our readiness to set forth and do it again. The most important and, for a time, I suspect the most influential pop culture figure in the early eighties was Rambo, a cartoonlike soldier played by the actor Sylvester Stallone. Stallone's movies implied that we had lost in Vietnam because the politicians had not let the military win and then went on to demean those who had fought there by suggesting that one actor with powerful deltoid muscles could take out a whole regiment of North Vietnamese infantry, played by dopey Asian cartoon figures left over from World War II movies. President Reagan was a professed admirer of Rambo's manly deeds. Indeed, during the last decade, a time when the lessons of Vietnam remained in front of us, still unacknowledged, we went through an odd period of almost hysterical jingoism; our rhetoric grew more strident, and our defense budget escalated, with the result that we savaged our own economy. We did not buy greater security, nor did we make ourselves militarily stronger. In five years President Reagan took us from a deficit of $78.9 billion to one of $221 billion and made us the greatest debtor nation in the history of mankind. Arguably that was artificial (or unusable) strength purchased at the expense of real strength—the viability and integrity of the American economic system. As Paul Kennedy has pointed out, the geometrically increasing kinds and numbers of modern weapons mean that the wise leader has to make skillful choices because one can no longer order everything on the list. The Reagan administration in its first term, Kennedy noted, spent some 75 percent more on new aircraft than Jimmy Carter did, yet it bought only 9 percent more planes.

Empire obscures reality not only at the level where the peons of empire are employed but worse, it obscures finally at the nerve center where the giants of empire govern.

If the first blow to the economy had come with the relatively limited inflation of the Vietnam War, the first oil shock in 1973 accelerated it. By 1972 the American economy, unlike that of other industrialized nations, had become not so much accustomed to cheap oil as addicted to it. In 1950 a gallon of gas had cost about twenty-seven cents at the pump, twenty cents of it for the gas itself; twenty-three years later, although energy was expensive elsewhere in the world (particularly in Europe, where energy discipline was enforced by extremely heavy taxes at the pump), America still lived in an energy dreamworld. The price of a gallon at the pump was only thirty-seven cents, twenty-six cents of that for the gas itself, the rest for taxes.

In October 1973 Egypt struck against Israel in what was called the Yom Kippur War; the war temporarily united the Arabs against those who supported Israel. In the process the Arab oil producers sent the price of oil skyrocketing, from three to twelve dollars a barrel.

Six years later the Shah's fall from power signaled the West's loss of control over Middle Eastern oil. The price again skyrocketed and revealed more starkly than ever the vulnerability of American industry. As I write, thousands of American troops lie in combat readiness, ringing Iraq in preparation for a war that no one seems to want, and to which there seems to be no advantageous outcome except the immediate punishment of an ugly dictator and the destruction of his war machine. But even if we win that war, we may lose in more subtle and complicated ways.

I am hardly an expert on the Middle East, but it is clear to me that the Cold War distorted American policy in this region, as it did in so many others. I don't mean to say that we saw it only as a platform for the Cold War; in the very beginning, had we thought of nothing but realpolitik, we might never have sponsored Israel, since it was clearly going to cost us dearly with the Arabs and give the Russians a good deal of room in which to maneuver.

But in the 1967 war, the Israelis proved themselves militarily (at the same time that America was performing with considerably less skill in Vietnam), and we began to see them as a powerful Western military force in the region. In the words of Joe Alsop, Israel was the only barrier between Nasser and Saudi oil.

This is true also of how we came to see Iran. At first we had tried to control the Shah's grandiosity and limit his annual shopping lists for Pentagon goodies. Kissinger, though, saw the Shah as the Western ally who could dominate the region, and

71

gave him everything he wanted. That policy might have made sense in terms of global Cold War alignments, but because of historic Arab fears of Persian aggression, it did nothing to make the region itself more stable. Rather, it helped raise the ante of armament and encouraged the Shah's egomania. In so doing, we may have helped separate the Shah from the realities of his people. For all the armament we supplied, he finally fell to forces from within, without a shot being fired.

American policy alone was not responsible for escalating tensions in the Middle East; every move we made was matched by the Soviets. But the steady increase of arms brought neither of the Cold War giants increased influence in the region.

As this policy in Iran failed, a new dynamic developed: The Shah's successors hated us and we, in turn, became enraged at them for what they did at our embassy. Inevitably, our policy tilted toward Iraq in the Iraq-Iran war. We argued that Iraq was the lesser of two evils because the Ayatollah wanted to take Iran backward in time, and Saddam Hussein wanted to take Iraq forward. The result is that we find ourselves on the brink of an unwanted war in an arena where we are at a considerable disadvantage.

Another moment of great symbolic importance involving America's signature industry came early in the Reagan administration, when we set a limit on how many cars the Japanese could export to us. In the American Century we did not buy cars made by an Asian nation half our size, whose goods we had so long scorned. The Japanese assault had actually been coming for some fifteen years, in cameras, steel, ships, and television sets. Now in the most important of America's industries we had asked for help, not just because Japanese cars were cheaper or smaller than ours but largely because they were better made. We found this hard to accept. Lee Iacocca, on some occasions when he is feeling sorry for himself, likes to complain about the uneven football field, as if we were playing uphill. But the truth, despite Japanese protectionism, is that for the first time since World War II the football field is level—that is, it no longer tilts in our favor. We have dissipated the enormous head start we had, and other nations have caught up with us. Some of that is inevitable; it was unrealistic to expect any nation to remain as dominating and powerful as America was.

We are barely beginning to come to terms with the downside of economic hegemony. As Naohiro Amaya once said to me, there was a certain danger that came from a national wealth too readily and almost unconsciously derived. Not all things that seemed to be blessings, he said, were blessings. We were so rich that a certain standard of living was built into our expectations. Eventually our political system was rooted in those expectations. It became the responsibility of the politicians rather than ourselves as citizens to produce that standard of living. As our monopoly period ended, we have done an extremely poor job of adapting to a new more Spartan age in a harsher, more competitive (and unsentimental) world. Our attempts to find a new discipline seem unconvincing indeed: Ford's WIN buttons and Carter's speech telling us that what was happening was the moral equivalent of war and then not telling us how to go out and fight it.

For some fifteen or twenty years we should have picked up signs that we were going down the wrong track, that our political expectations and our economic realities were diverging. The failure of the government to do honest budgeting during the Vietnam War was the first sign. The failure to deal with a dramatically changed world energy price in both 1973 and 1979 by not taxing citizens heavily at the pump was another. If there was an early example of a paralysis of political will, it was here: we were afraid to tax our own people honestly, so in effect we allowed the Arabs to tax us.

In the fall of 1990 Congress and President Bush were mired in a sad political shadow dance over taxation, yet another example of how we seem unable to move toward the new era, unable even to discuss our changed economic circumstances. As we edge ever closer to forced budgetary action, the object seems not so much to face the future as to leave as few fingerprints as possible on any legislation. The frail package tentatively agreed upon hardly seems to be the answer—it is barely even a beginning. Although we stand virtually alone in the Western world in our failure to tax gasoline adequately, the new budget calls for an increase of a mere five to fourteen cents at the pump. Clearly, despite all the warnings that this is not merely an economic issue, but also one of national security, we remain unwilling to impose any discipline upon ourselves that demands a change in our life-styles.

We became skillful at coming up with new economic measures to loosen traditional financial restraints, to make the economy appear healthier than it really was. We became an increasingly profligate nation, as Martin Lipton has noted. The banks, rather than being disciplined at critical times, looked for new fields to use their money and talked enthusiastically of a sexy new world of Eurodollars and petrodollars and were freed from the traditional restraints of depending upon their own reserves. The more they could lend out, the better. We came up with subtle and not so subtle ways of creating artificial means, not so much to stimulate growth as to resemble it. The savings and loan companies decided to go on the fast track, the restraints on their investment policies removed by a sympathetic and amiable government, which simply passed responsibility for bad investments from the heads of the S&Ls to the taxpayers. We began to glorify the art of leverage. The new heroes were the men who made deals rather than those who made products. We invented increasingly lax means of financing—junk bonds—in order to allow ourselves to live above our means. The idea that there might be some limits to this, that there was something indecent to it all, that it was mostly based on taking over companies, getting your share out quickly, and saddling the company with immense debt did not seem to bother many people. We witnessed a split-level economy, more stagnant than we wanted to admit (its very stagnant quality offering raiders wondrous targets), and a tiny handful of people making fortunes without any connection to true productivity. Their fellow citizens looked on with amazement and held on to the unlikely idea that they, too, would get their fair shares.

How quickly it all goes when it's built on sand. As I write, Boesky has already been to jail, Milken awaits a sentence, and Donald Trump's empire is in the hands of his bankers (the key to the Trump success, while it lasted, was that New York City was in such bad shape that it gave him a $160 million tax benefit for his glitzy projects).

The result, of course, was not greater productivity but a major leap in wealth for the already wealthy. As Kevin Phillips has noted, between 1981 and 1988 the net worth of *Fortune* magazine's four hundred richest Americans nearly tripled. Studies by the Brookings Institute showed that the share of national income going to the wealthiest 1 percent of the population rose from 8.1 percent in 1981 to 14.7 percent in 1986. This was taking place as America loaded itself with debt and other nations passed us in per capita income.

We have not yet come to accept that we do not set the standard for excellence in productivity anymore. There are other nations with different systems, different educational systems, different labor systems, and different systems of capital formation, who do things as well as or better than Americans. There are other countries that place a higher value on education and other countries that reinvest more in their capital structures and in R&D. There are countries where important companies derive their capital from banks rather than from a volatile equity market, and therefore, their managers can plan in long-range terms. Their companies often make higher-quality goods than ours do. We had, it turned out, picked up many bad habits over some thirty years of affluence. We were less competitive than we thought we were, domestically and internationally. Our largest companies failed to modernize and hid behind their very size.

Even now, as the Japanese pour ever more money into R&D, even as the technology in many of their industrial companies is now for the first time better than ours, we cling to the notion that our good luck will hold. We believe outdated clichés that we are more original thinkers than they, better inventors than they, and that their only skill is to take a given invention and make it better than ours. Certainly in the past there was some truth to such generalizations, but there is already evidence that the Japanese are now, in many areas, doing original industrial, electronic, and ceramic research that is ahead of ours.

As we prepare for a competition that has already started, we are going to have a very difficult time because unlike some of our competitors, we are now, more than any other nation in the world, a truly pluralistic society. In some of our major urban centers, we have become a combination of first and third world populations. We *thought* we were pluralistic at the turn of the last century, when America was surging into its industrial prime. That America was a powerful society waiting to be bonded; it was produced by an east to west migration across the Atlantic, and though the languages of the new immigrants were different, the cultures were essentially the same. The gap in values between those who arrived and those who were already here was much smaller than either group realized. Today's pluralism is far more complicated. It is touched by race and the ravages of slavery and by people deprived of education for more than a century. The centrist covenants that held America together in the past are shakier, and today's disenfranchised are more alienated.

We seem to those overseas a different power from that of thirty years ago—less confident, less dynamic, more insular, more churlish. We blame others for our faults, most notably the slowdown of our economy. We are angry at the Japanese for their trade policies (certainly some of them are unattractive), but the Japanese are doing only what other nations would do in the same situation: maximizing their own position. We choose to ignore some of the most important reasons that Japan does so well, among them that the Japanese reinvest more readily in capital equipment and create new industrial facilities at virtually twice the rate we do (roughly 10 percent to 4.9 percent). The concept of reciprocity in trade seems alien to the Japanese, but even in the areas where we have a legitimate case against them, we make it poorly. There are several reasons for this, and one of them is the need to live over our heads. We have become dependent upon the Japanese to buy our treasury bills. We are not very good at our new relationship of financial dependence. Japan, in effect, must balance our budget for us (if anything, some of our most important financiers have become more nervous now about the shakiness of Japan's stock market than our own because we know how shaky ours actually is). We therefore are in the ironic position of lecturing to the Japanese about their being fairer in their trade policy (an absolutely legitimate position) but of being so ill disciplined ourselves that we need to sidle over to them at the end of the lecture and ask if they can lend us some more money.

America needs to reexamine our inflated view of our world role and our inflated view of how well our own economy works. We have yet to come to terms with the true limits of our power and to reconcile our national debate to those limits. The case could be made that as Gorbachev has to unlearn the orthodoxy of whether or not the Soviet Union worked, so should a contemporary American President unlearn most of our long-held assumptions about how viable our economy is and ask what we can do to forge a strong economy into the next century.

IV

THE JAPANESE WERE NEVER PART of the Cold War, but they were ideally positioned to exploit it (that is, to be a part of it without being a part of it). Their nationalism was instinctive. To the outsider the Japanese seem a nation apart, a people who, because of the distinct nature of their history, geography, and language, prefer to think of themselves as a race.

The anticommunism of their ruling class was visceral, and they were glad, by and large, that America played the role it did in the postwar Pacific, but their essential purpose was always about Japan, never about some grand alliance. They have a singular sense of their own destiny. We cajoled and pressured them into doing exactly what they intended to do all along. We believed the Japanese were allies, that we shared similar goals (as well as enemies). Now, as we begin to face the true realities and intricacies of the relationship (on such issues as sharing technology on fighter planes), we both realize how little we know of each other.

Essentially the Japanese success is their own. They modernized on their own terms, adjusting in ways that felt comfortable to them, blending the needs of the present and the future while holding on to as much of the past as possible. Theirs was first an economic or industrial modernization and only then, reluctantly, a social and political one. They brilliantly took traditional Japanese forms and adapted them to the modern workplace. They were at once completely modern yet surprisingly feudal. "The electronic tribe" the writer Donald Richie has called them. In the years after the war their personal and national goals seemed to mesh perfectly, and they were able to attain in peacetime a level of nationalism and sacrifice that other nations could summon only in times of war.

Japan, more than any other nation I can think of, was the beneficiary of our empire. In different ways the wars in Korea and Vietnam helped the Japanese economy immeasurably. At the start of the Korean War any number of Japan's largest industrial companies, having fought bloody battles with left-wing unions, were near bankruptcy. The economy was ill disciplined; inflation was rampant. Even before the Korean War broke out, the rise of tensions in Europe between the West and the Soviets and the decline of Chiang's forces on the mainland of China, forced *Washington* (not MacArthur) to change the essential tilt of American policy toward Japan. There had been a good deal of zaibatsu bashing in the early days of the occupation. That was soon over. The zaibatsu would be allowed to regroup in different ways and in different garb. The purges of wartime businessmen stopped. The radicalism of the leftist unions was no longer tolerated. Most important of all, the runaway inflation that seemed to perpetuate the wartime devastation and pessimism was ended.

During the Korean War Japan became a critical supply base for the American forces in Korea—for trucks and jeeps and napalm. Korea provided the boost that Japan's struggling industrial forces needed to right themselves. They never ran in the red again. With the tacit approval of the Americans, the Japanese ruling class changed the nature of trade unions; the leadership came no longer from the workers themselves but from middle management. It was the perfect example of how the Japanese took the goals of the Americans and fitted them to their own needs. There was now industrial harmony for the workers, but at least some of it was involuntary; there were no other options.

The years of the Vietnam War—1965–1975—cover the true surge of the Japanese economy. My clearest memory from 1967, pre-Tet, was thousands of Americans wandering around Saigon in combat gear and hundreds of Japanese businessmen in their civilian clothes doing business in the city's best hotels and eating at new Japanese restaurants. What seemed like thousands and thousands of young Vietnamese men and women were riding around on Honda motorbikes. We were obsessed with the Cold War and now the hot war, but the Japanese were obsessed with commerce.

One incident will suffice to show the different visions of the two nations at that particular moment. It was a conflict that took place within the small American community in Tokyo in the mid-sixties. Frustrated senior American businessmen there complained that the Japanese, who they knew were in the midst of a prolonged boom, kept their own markets closed, even as they set their sights on exporting their way to becoming a world-class industrial superpower. The top American diplomats at the American Embassy barely listened to them. They had a different agenda for Japan, one set in Washington by the people at Defense and State: to use whatever leverage we had in Tokyo to keep the Japanese lined up as a rhetorical ally during Vietnam. The commercial attaché at the embassy, who represented the American businessmen, did not have the clout to intervene. The Japanese, as the saying then went, had to be kept on the team. At the moment we had maximum leverage in Japan, we chose not to use it. The American business community was furious. It was the classic decision of the Cold War to keep the Japanese aligned as allies in Vietnam—a course they would have followed anyway—rather than confront them on their domestic trade policies and ruffle their feathers. It was an odd collision of perceived national interests with real national interests, and perceived national interests always won in the Cold War.

Japan's challenge to the American economy began during the escalation of the Vietnam War. Yet the challenge was barely perceived by a nation so absolutely absorbed by war. In Japan an immense mercantile force was gathering, and we chose not to see it. Japan was in some degree to America during its two Asian wars what American was to Europe during its two great ill-fated wars. Visiting Tokyo in the eighties, knowing how the Japanese had prospered in part because of the war, I had a sense of history's repeating itself, of how an Englishman or a Frenchman must have felt visiting America in the late forties.

I do not think the Japanese ever thought in terms of a Capitalist bloc or Communist bloc. They thought, as befits a nation where the sense of nationalism is so powerful, always of the greater good of Japan. Their economy in the end represented a form of state-guided communal capitalism. While the communal society failed in Eastern Europe because it was an equal misery distributor instead of an equal benefits distributor, it succeeded in its capitalist manifestation in Japan. There it fitted the historic needs and traditions of the country, a poor land where, if the rewards were too great at the top, the poverty would be too great at the bottom. There was nothing very ideological about modern Japanese capitalism, for the Japanese had the most pragmatic of societies. Everything was based on the best use of a nation's limited resources. Like the citizens of most nations, the Japanese might be prisoners of their own national myths, but they were never prisoners of ideology.

After World War II Japan's defense budget was negligible, and because of that, its economy remained finely tuned, and there was little waste. Less went in at one end and more came out at the other than in any comparable developed economy. It poured its best scientists into the consumer economy rather than into the defense or the space industry.

I think of Japan not so much as a political system but as a condition. If Japan is a democracy, it is a democracy with a condition that is, for a people aspiring to national greatness, essentially authoritarian. The harshness of its condition and the broad public acceptance of the limits it imposed set the limits of freedom in contemporary Japan. Whereas we in America, in our endlessly bountiful land with its essentially comfortable climate, were conditioned to think that there would always be more, the Japanese grew up in a country where the very physical nature of the land suggested that there might easily be less. Anyone in Japan who uses too much, whether it be food, or money, or personal freedom of speech, is not merely perceived to be taking too much from the nation but is presumed to be taking it at the expense of others. These limits are set not merely in the case of natural resources but in terms of personal freedoms. As Amaya notes, sardines packed in a tin cannot be too individualistic. Japanese culture carries inherent standards of sacrifice.

Even the deliberate modesty of the Japanese, whereby one person never takes credit for any achievement and never tries to call attention to himself or herself but instead always talks about the good of the company, is, I suspect, an outgrowth of the same condition. It is as if in a country this poor, even ego must be rationed, and if one person has too much or expends too much of it, he is stealing from others. Once at a press conference held by Sony to unveil a new product, the veteran American journalist Bernard Krisher asked Akio Morita, the head of the company, who had actually invented the product. "Krishersan, you have been in our country long enough to know not to ask a question like that," Morita answered.

I do not think of the Japanese as a nimble people. Subtle, perhaps, but not nimble. They have the most rigidly hierarchical system I have ever seen. Above all, Japan is not a society where people act on instinct. Everything is carefully considered. Often it is considered better not to act than to act precipitously. A simple answer from an ordinary person in middle management is often hard to get. A great deal of effort goes into not making a mistake. But if the Japanese are not nimble as people, they nonetheless have a nimble economy.

They have an extremely sophisticated upper bureaucracy, they have a well-motivated, well-educated work force, and they have enormous capital resources. Thus, as the world economy changes, they can adapt and shift talented people from one field to another, and they can shift capital reserves from one field to another. In the last decade they have moved the thrust of their economy from core industries to high technology. In the last two or three years they have slightly slowed the rate of their capital reinvestment and have greatly increased their investment in the critical factor for success in high technology: R&D. All this is done with some measure of guidance from their high bureaucracy. Because of the nature of their condition, the Japanese are not a very sentimental people; they believe that it may be all right in a country as inherently wealthy as America to make mistakes and not to worry about long-range planning, but they also believe that for them, a failure to plan, to sense the future, would be fatal. Japan is not a nation that likes surprises.

At night in Tokyo the conversations often turn to two subjects: the alleged softness of the next generation of Japanese and the rise of the Koreans. The two subjects are, of course, intertwined. In these conversations the young are relentlessly criticized for being spoiled (though they have had to work far harder to get into Japan's best schools than those who went before them—those doing the talking), for their desire to drive expensive cars, for not working as late at the office as the preceding generation, and for spending vast amounts of yen on vacations in Hawaii. Worst of all, more often than not, they grew up with air conditioning and central heating. Can a generation that has had air conditioning and central heating be truly trusted to run a country that depends on its sense of adversity to guide it through a perilous world? Or will they catch what the Japanese call, when Americans are not present, the American disease? The talk then switches to the Koreans, the (often) hated and dreaded Koreans but also the respected Koreans (who themselves refer to the Japanese as the lazy Asians). The Koreans are now grudgingly admired because they are doing very Japanese-like things (producing good steel, ships, and cars) and because their young people are working harder and longer with fewer complaints.

The Koreans pose a threat that the Americans or even the West Germans do not. The Americans or the West Germans are not likely to reinvent themselves as the children of greater hardship. The Koreans, however, are another matter. The Koreans do not have to reinvent themselves to be poorer. The Koreans *are* poorer. They represent not only a poorer nation (that is, a place where workers' salaries are much smaller) but, more significantly, a culture of greater adversity, a people who have known greater hardship and oppression than the Japanese, indeed, oppression inflicted by the Japanese themselves. The Koreans make the Japanese doubly uneasy.

If America in the postwar years became a *political* society, one where there was an assumption of the essential health and bountiful quality of the American economy, then Japan by contrast was an *economic* society, where wealth had to be renewed each day by the nation's most talented people. Politics is a secondary business in Japan, and that means journalism is a tertiary business, its being a field that derives from politics.

In America, because we are so political, virtually everyone fights to have access to the elite television shows and print media, and because of technological breakthroughs, journalism has become ever more important in the last twenty-five years. Actually the last group to learn how to use the media has been the business or managerial class. In Japan, where journalism holds a less exalted position, a visiting American is constantly surprised to find that when he visits a television station or a magazine, an envelope containing several thousand yen is handed to him. He has been paid for the favor of doing something he intended to do anyway.

Because Japan is economically oriented, its most talented young college graduates aspire to serve the nation by working in the high bureaucracy on economic matters. When I think of the most celebrated Japanese figures of the postwar era, I see Soichuro Honda and Akio Morita, not any of the nation's politicians. Japan's national security apparatus, in contrast with America's, is an economic one. The Ministry of Finance and the Ministry of International Trade (MITI) form, with the Ministry of Foreign Affairs, a powerful trinity within the bureaucracy. It monitors first and foremost Japan's economic relations with the rest of the world or, perhaps more accurately, its political relations as determined by its economic interests. By contrast, the weakest voice, indeed a virtually nonexistent voice in the formulation of American foreign policy, has been that of the Commerce Department, which represents or is supposed to represent American business interests there.

In America much of the energy of the society has gone into politics, which has focused largely on determining America's path in the Cold War (in the Kennedy Cabinet, for example, all the good jobs were in foreign policy and national security). Likewise, the journalists of the postwar generation, men and women

86

now in their fifties and early sixties, were by and large economic illiterates (I include myself before I took what was in effect a six-year crash course in trying to define why the Japanese challenge to the American core economy had been so successful). Our best reporters came to prominence by dint of their reporting either on the Cold War or on political and social issues: civil rights; Vietnam; Watergate. Almost none of them rose to the top by covering business news, and the weakest sections of our newspapers and magazines were until quite recently the business sections.

Our major columnists reflect our domestic bias in their training as well; they are conditioned by the nature of op-ed page rules, one on the left, one on the right, a reflection of our norms and our divisions, rather than the norms and the divisions of the real world. As such, few of our commentators can deal with Japan's ascent since it defies the traditional definitions of American ideology (liberal and conservative). It is national and cultural. That having been said, it is just as hard to describe the comparable erosion in America and the weakening of covenants in ideological definitions.

Japan has marked the beginning of the new century by coming forward as a powerful new international player, but even more important, it has given the world a new definition of economic power. The American Century resulted from a time when a nation's economic power came from its sheer physical size, its natural wealth, and a willingness of the government not to put too many obstacles in the way of economic development.

Japan, a nation with no natural resources at all, has achieved economic excellence by maximizing the productivity of its citizens through education. As Secretary of State George Shultz noted at the time of the Iran-contra hearings, economic wealth in communications once existed because a nation had a great deal of copper under the soil. But who, he added, needs copper in an age of fiber optics?

Education, therefore, is critical in the new age. Before, men wearing blue-collar shirts did the work at machines; in the new age, men with higher levels of education help run and repair machines that do the work. In America now, at a modern factory, the ideal worker is someone who not only has a high school degree and a high level of competence in math but has served in the air force or gone to a junior college.

As the nature of economic power changed, so the rules for economic success were changing. In the simpler days of American hegemony, bigger was always better. Size of company and scale of production were the keys to success. General Motors was the classic example of the successful corporation of the period; in an age of de facto monopoly when size was power, it obliterated potential competitors. Then came the new challenge from the Japanese. Bigger was no longer necessarily better. Better meant a higher-quality product. If the world economy was a more crowded place, then the advantage was held by the more disciplined society, which wasted less and used its resources, human and natural, more carefully and skillfully.

When I think of that drive for excellence and the sense of personal obligation that it so often represents, I think often of Kazuo Inamori. Inamori is the head of a spectacularly successful company in Kyoto called Kyocera (Kyoto Ceramics), and while he is not as well known in America as Soichuro Honda of Honda or Akio Morita of Sony, I suspect someday soon he will be. If Honda was a Japanese Henry Ford of the automobile industry and Morita (although less of a lab and factory man) a comparable figure in electronics, then Inamori is Ford's lineal descendant in support systems for high technology. He is a man who has placed his company on the leading edge of technology. Nothing bores him more than things in which he has already succeeded. "What we like to do next," he says, "is what people tell us we can never do." A recent poll in the *Nihon Keizai Shimbun,* the *Wall Street Journal* of Japan, showed that while the average Japanese citizen thought Sony would be the most successful Japanese company in the next century, the average Japanese businessman thought Kyocera was the one to watch. Its stunning success in the last twenty-five years was a by-product of the semiconductor revolution. Suddenly there were significant new uses for ceramics as a base in high technology because it was resistant to heat yet did not conduct electricity. Kyocera's product was the best in the world; as the demand for ceramic parts expanded, Kyocera gained a reputation in both America and Japan as the highest-quality supplier of them. That high quality and the originality of Kyocera's techniques resulted, as Inamori likes to point out, because unlike the heads of competing American and West German companies, he himself was always on the floor, overseeing the kilns and varying the mixes. As success came, Inamori did not sit back. He drove himself and those around him even harder. Now the company rushes ahead to find new applications for ceramics—ceramic teeth, ceramic replacements for human body parts, ceramic auto engines, ceramic knives, and ceramic bases for solar heating. "We are," says his friend and colleague Richard Nagai, "the leaders in the new Stone Age."

It is difficult to figure out how old Inamori is by looking at him. There is not a gray hair on his head. His face is completely unlined. One would never guess that this is a man who pushes himself to his limits, who usually slept in his office during the first two decades of his company's history, and whose nickname was Mr. A.M. because he never left work before 3:00 or 4:00 A.M. In fact, he is 58 years old. He is, according to his colleague Nagai, a dreamer. "But he does not dream up long-term visions. He dreams in tiny increments. If he has the idea of making teeth from ceramics, he will try that, and only then, if that succeeds, will he dream the next step," says Nagai. "Only then will he dream of making other body parts. His dreams are very practical." Or as Inamori himself adds, "Most industrialists don't dream, and most dreamers don't manufacture things, so I am very lucky."

By Japanese standards Inamori has always been something of a rebel. His father was a small printer in Kagoshima, successful enough to buy a home in a snobbish samurai neighborhood where the Inamori family was never quite accepted. One thing that Inamori realized about his father years later was that he always repaired his printing machines himself. Inamori's mother berated her husband for this, for she felt it was beneath him, but it gave him pleasure; he believed that the machines were an extension of himself. Therefore, he should repair them himself. When Kazuo applied for junior high school, his father was supposed to write down on his application which class his family came from. Most of his friends' parents wrote down "samurai." His father put down "ordinary citizen." Kazuo did not get into one of Japan's elite colleges, Todai or Keio. The University of Osaka, where he wanted to go, turned him down. Instead, he went to Kagoshima, a lunch box school, as the Japanese call it. By the rigidly hierarchical system of Japan, that should have determined his career; because he had not gone to a good school, he would not end up at a good company, and even at a lesser company he would be a limited success. At first that seemed to be his fate. Though he had been graduated in the top of his class, the big companies were not interested in him. He ended up at a small ceramics company in Kyoto, where he was treated as something of a second-class citizen. At his new company the class divisions were immediately obvious, and it was clear who was destined to succeed and who was not.

He came to realize much later that he was unconsciously part of the same snobbishness that he came to hate. For even

90

though he had not been to one of Japan's more prestigious universities, he was nevertheless a college man, and he believed that less well-educated men did the real work underneath the successful men, who, he believed, should not get their hands dirty. Yet working with Inamori on the floor was a senior person. He was not well educated, but he loved his work. He brought perfection to even the smallest tasks, down to how he cleaned the ball and the mill when he was mixing ceramics. There was a purity to his actions, a love of working as an end in itself. This man is like a Zen monk, thought Inamori. The art is in the doing, in the making. "I watched him day after day and saw the pleasure that even the tiniest detail gave him. Suddenly I realized that the pleasure in work did not come from being an overseer or a boss, but the pleasure was in the doing. Mixing ceramics is an art, and it is not a simple art. You have to adapt and change all the time if you are trying to get consistent quality. In mixing you can mix brilliantly or you can mix carelessly, and he was doing it brilliantly, and he was taking such pleasure from it. Up until then I thought I was above things like mixing, and from then on I knew I was not. I realized that if I was above mixing, I should not be in a ceramics company."

Early in his career Inamori was part of a team trying to create an insulating part for an electronic gun for cathode tubes. He was the only member of the team who had not gone to Kyoto University, yet he came to realize that he was the most original team member. He was the leader of the group, in all but recognition by superiors. At the very moment that they made a breakthrough, there was a strike (this was in the late fifties, when some of Japan's unions were still radical). It appeared likely that the company, which was barely in the black, was going to be shut down. Along with about twenty workers Inamori stayed on and continued to make the piece that was a key part for the Matsushita Company. He was, in effect, a strikebreaker.

He believed that the company's future depended on the ability to supply the part. He and others lived in the plant; Inamori smuggled food in for them and finished parts were smuggled out to Matsushita. In time he was tried by a people's court as "a running dog for capitalism" but was acquitted when he chose to defend himself. He was not enraged by the union leaders' trial of him; he could understand that. What enraged him was the company's response. For his loyalty the company tried to reward him with extra money. He was insulted. His loyalty was not so much to the company as to the work, to make the piece better. He turned the bonus down. "They never understood. They thought I was doing it for them, but what I wanted was the piece itself to be better. I had told all those who stayed and worked with me that we were doing something creative and beautiful. I said that if the piece was better, then the company, I was sure, would be better. And then they wanted to give me money for this! They never understood." As the project achieved even greater success, he was told by his superiors that he would have to leave the team because although he had contributed considerably, he was not from a first-rate university. "They wanted to give my work to their favorite sons!" He was furious and decided to resign from the company. In 1958, with ten thousand dollars borrowed from friends and a hundred-thousand-dollar line of credit, he founded Kyocera. That was unusual. Japan is not a country where a man lightly leaves a larger company to start his own.

He had no grand ambitions. He wanted merely to keep doing his research, to keep working on the floor and trying to find the perfect mix for each new part. If he kept working on the floor, he was sure, he would find the answers to the future. The way for their company to succeed, he told his assembled new employees, was to try to have a perfect day at work. If they did that, soon the perfect day would become a perfect week and a perfect month and a perfect year. But it had to begin with a perfect day.

His company was successful from the first. But it had a hard time breaking into the big time because Japan's larger companies had formed an old-boy network; new companies could not get sizable contracts. That blocked Kyocera's ability to expand in Japan.

So Inamori decided to come to the United States to see if he could buy some American patents and upgrade his business. A modest young man of thirty with very little money, only ten dollars a day to spend, he arrived in 1962. Almost thirty years later he could remember Tad's, a steakhouse in Times Square where a steak dinner was $1.19, or $1.49 with salad. He was at once scared and humbled by the size of the United States. He believed excellence and perfection to be all around him. Nagai, who worked for a Japanese trading company and was based in New York at the time, was assigned to take him around. He was impressed by Inamori's youth (Nagai could not find him at the airport at first because he had assumed that a managing director would be a venerable gentleman of at least sixty, not a scared young man of thirty). It was quite touching, Nagai thought, this young Japanese come to the land of the masters, anxious to visit American companies and buy their patents so he could improve his business in Japan.

As they visited company after company, an epiphany occurred, first to Nagai and only later, because he was less worldly, to Inamori. "His technology and his products were already better than theirs, but he did not realize it," Nagai said. "All of this, the great new land, overwhelmed him, and he was in such awe at first that he could not believe his own quality was superior. But I could see it; I did not know that much about ceramics, but I could see that his products were better than theirs, and I could see their eyes going through the ceiling. Here he was in his humble way apologizing for the quality of his goods, and they were *dazzled*. They could not believe how good he was." Finally Nagai took Inamori aside and told him he was already ahead of the Americans, that he should be coming here to sell his products rather than to license their technology. What struck Nagai, along with the excellence of Inamori's product, was his passion. "All he would talk about when we were together was his belief in what a company should be, what its obligations were. I'm not with an engineer, I finally decided; I'm with some kind of missionary."

With that Inamori began to sell his products in the United States. America was far ahead of the rest of the world in the early sixties in computers and computer chips; therefore, anyone wanting to sell ceramics for high technology uses had to come here. Kyocera soon became the best manufacturer and creator of ceramics for modern uses in the world. It soon became a primary supplier to America's most advanced companies.

Inamori was amazed at how open the Americans were in contrast with Japanese companies back home. His first big breakthrough came from Texas Instruments. In 1963 Texas Instruments was looking for an insulating rod for the base for a silicon transistor. Inamori received the specifications and worked on them. The initial results were good enough for Kyocera to become one of two companies competing for the contract. The other was Rosenthal, a West German company that Inamori greatly respected. Inamori was sure of one thing, though, as he worked day and night, changing the mix, trying to improve and sustain the quality: The head of Rosenthal was not in front of the kiln twenty hours a day. "We got the contract," he said, "because we were so good at mixing and baking, because the top people in the company were in front of the kilns all the time, and they could control the variances and keep the quality consistent, which is very hard in ceramics."

This success opened the door for others. Soon he got an order from Fairchild. A year later he heard that Sony was going to produce the first transistor products for radios, so he went to Sony. The people there treated him cavalierly as expected. But he

94

was more confident now; he was no longer the poor little boy from Kagoshima but the modern Japanese businessman who supplied great American companies with delicate parts, whose quality and consistency had been praised by the Americans themselves. As such he pushed his case with greater audacity than he might have in the past. What Sony needed was a ceramic base the size of a cigarette butt, about 0.5 millimeters thick, with two holes in it and with a cut in the middle. It was an unusually difficult assignment because the part was so thin. Established manufacturing processes would tend to split it. Yet Inamori regarded this as a critical order; there had to be an innovative way to produce the part. He and his staff brainstormed. Then one day he thought of spaghetti: They would mix the powders like dough and press it through tubes as if it were pasta and slice the chips off rather than press them down. Simple as it was, it worked. Susumu Yoshida, a Sony executive, demanded to know how he had done it. "We did it as if we were making pasta," Inamori answered. "That's too primitive," Yoshida said. "You can't do that." Yoshida demanded a tour of the factory. At first Inamori refused, but it became clear that he would not get the contract unless he permitted Sony's people to see the process. It was, Yoshida finally acknowledged, the most primitive state-of-the-art technique he had ever seen.

With that, Kyocera's reputation was made. Inamori, if anything, became more zealous. He was terrified that he would now become complacent and lose his edge. He had visited great companies in America and had been surprised to see that their floors were dirty and that their employees smoked at work. He knew of Japanese companies where men had isolated themselves once they had become successful. He had been successful, Inamori decided, not because he and the others around him were so brilliant but because they had never left the factory floor. He promoted only those men who were creative on the floor. "The people who

95

are running the company today," he likes to point out, "are all people who got their hands dirty working on the floor five and ten years ago. We do not separate the abstract from the practical."

Not surprisingly Kyocera now has a reputation in Japan as a formidable company that demands exceptional sacrifice. Inamori drives himself and those around him relentlessly. He complains often that the young do not work as hard as the last generation. These days many of the best graduates of Japan's engineering schools do not want to work on the line in companies like his, he says, they want to stay in Tokyo and work at white-collar jobs in financial houses. Their hands, he says, are always clean. He teases a young man who is working at his side, who is in public relations. "Look at Watanabe here. He should be down on the floor learning our business, and he is in public relations. This new generation!" Watanabe does not respond to this. He has clearly heard it before. "College graduates," Inamori continues, "are too theoretical. They think that factories are distant and unimportant. They need to learn the importance of *making* something and of *producing* something. Only then are they valuable." He and some of his top executives were slightly wounded a few years ago when some of the professors at Japan's top universities complained that Kyocera was working their best graduates too hard and, worse, *using them in blue-collar jobs.* More recently the universities have learned to send Kyocera only young men of such character that they will not be worn down by the company's high demands. Now the company gets about 130 new scientists coming in each year from the colleges, and only 7 or 8 drop out. The culture of the company, after all, is not a secret.

This past year Kyocera celebrated its thirtieth anniversary. The company seemed more dynamic and successful than ever. It had become an international company, with five factories in America alone. The new Europe also beckoned. Inamori had no intention, he told his employees on the occasion of its anniversary, of turning the company over to his children; a company about science belonged to its scientists and workers. Fearing that he was no longer as original scientifically as he had once been, Inamori had passed the reins of the company over to the top technologist of the next generation. Still, the thought of a thirtieth anniversary stirred powerful memories in him and made him edgy, for there is a Japanese saying that the life of a company is thirty years, and then it starts to fall apart. As he hailed the anniversary, he thought of American Lava and his visit there almost thirty years ago. At that time American Lava, located in Chattanooga, Tennessee, was the foremost industrial ceramics company in the world. In Kyoto Inamori had read about it and had often envisioned it, for he thought it the place where he could learn the most. As a young man on his first trip to America, he had repeatedly asked to see people at American Lava, but his requests had been turned down. Nonetheless, he had pleaded with Nagai to take him to Chattanooga, where he insisted on going out to the plant and driving around its perimeter. Nagai had been amazed by the intensity of Inamori's concentration as he looked at the plant and counted the smokestacks. It was as if, thought Nagai, he were willing himself to see inside the plant, envisioning the factory and the workers, creating it in his own mind. Then he had thanked Nagai and was ready to go back to New York. The ensuing thirty years had not been good ones for America Lava. It had been bought and sold several times, and each time it had seemed to slip a little further away from its original purpose. Inamori believed that each new group of management cared ever less about ceramics. It was, Inamori thought, very easy, both in America and in Japan, to fall from grace.

V

OUR DILEMMA IS COMPLICATED. IT is the inevitable product of three generations of affluence, which in turn created a culture of high expectations, which in turn created politics premised on high assumptions and high consumption.

What had started in the early fifties as a sense of possibilities gradually became expectations and then finally entitlement. Those who have memories of a poorer pre-World War II America, one touched by the Depression, where people (and the nation) had to make choices about spending, are older and increasingly a minority. Whereas the grandparents bought nothing on credit and were appalled by the idea of owing anything, their sons and daughters started coming to the conclusion that there was such a thing as a mortgage and that a little credit was acceptable. Now we have the current generation, which believes that living in the present and paying in the future is the best revenge, that those who pay with cash are fools, too stupid to take advantage of a government that so handsomely rewards buying on credit. Whenever we see someone in front of us at an airline ticket counter who is paying with cash, we make the immediate assumption that here is someone who is poor.

But our political debate does not accept the new equation, that the years of easy affluence are over. It turns on the idea that everything is as it used to be. We may be a debtor nation, the greatest in the history of mankind, but the national debt, like the trade imbalance with Japan, is not an issue that mobilizes people and sends them to the barricades. We have become a nation divided: Our political system is still based philosophically on the glory days of hegemony, but our economic (and social) system is stumbling clumsily in the early days of the new international economy. The result is a society oddly oblivious of its new realities, a people and a nation living above their heads, and politicians who dare not tell the truth to the population.

Voodoo economics, George Bush said in 1980 of Ronald Reagan's promise to do all existing things, increase defense spending and not increase taxes. Voodoo he said it was, and voodoo it turned out to be. Reagan's decision to cut taxes at that moment was, in the words of James Schlesinger, a former Secretary of Defense and head of the CIA, "the most irresponsible decision in American fiscal history," and the passage of a decade has not made his judgment look harsh. Schlesinger also predicted that the deficit would go to $150 billion. When Bush himself ran for President eight years later, the dilemma again faced the nation. How could we cut the deficit without raising taxes, as the President promised? "Read my lips," Bush said, and he was elected. Since then he has spent much of his time trying to mediate between the promises he made in his campaign and the realities he faces in governing.

The most interesting thing about the Reagan years, the aspect least commented on, was that Reagan was so poor a conservative. It was a stunning reversal of the image he had projected for his entire political life. "There was no connection at all between the image he projected as a true conservative and the substantive decisions of the government he professed to head," said Schlesinger, a quite conservative man himself. Rather than adjust America's spending to new realities, Schlesinger added, Reagan's fiscal and defense policies "adjusted our sights much higher than we could readily handle while at the same time reducing our capabilities to a point much lower." For the New Deal and the post-New Deal liberalism, which began in the thirties and ran all the way through the sixties, was fueled and sustained by America's emergence as a world power. By the seventies it was clear, both domestically and internationally, that the forces that had driven that particular America were running out of steam (in no small part, the reason Reagan was elected). America both as a nation and as a people would have to be more disciplined. It had to make harder choices; it needed to make certain sacrifices as it passed from one era to another; it needed to *conserve* in the classic sense of the word, as opposed to waste. I have always thought of conservatives as skeptics who saved for the future, spent within their means, and, above all, did not assure that things would always be as good as they were.

In the Reagan years we did not face the harsher new economic realities. Rather, we winked at them and went on a binge of spending. It was capitalism gone mad. The eighties, Pat Moynihan noted, was a decade in which we borrowed a trillion dollars from the Japanese and gave a very good party for ourselves. The Japanese were conservative. They were conservative because they saved, often at a rate four times greater than we did. As true productivity declined, we began to sell off the future to pay for the present. As we softened the dollar, American companies went on the market at bargain-basement prices. We were, said Warren Buffett, like a once-wealthy family whose life-style requires more than its annual earned wealth, who must sell off a little acreage every year until one day it wakes up to find out that it is no longer the owner of the manor but a tenant farmer.

Not surprisingly most Americans, faced with a new equation, wanted it both ways. They wanted a sort of no-fault patriotism—to keep enjoying the far greater personal freedoms and entitlements of the seventies and eighties with the vastly improved life-style and greater professional possibilities, while their neighbors were to revert to the more disciplined lives of the fifties. We were in effect a great free people anxious for everyone to start making sacrifices, except, of course, ourselves.

What we did not get from Reagan was what we needed most badly: a conservative education from his bully pulpit, introducing us to a real world that was gaining on us. The bluntness of Thatcher in her early years would have been preferable. Rather, he reinforced the illusion that we did not need to change. There was something oddly passive about his years: rhetoric separated from action and reality. The real world seemed to bore him. The most devastating portraits of him have been drawn, ironically, not by those in the allegedly liberal eastern press, presumed to be his sworn enemies, but in the books by his closest aides—for example, Alexander Haig, Donald Regan, and Peggy Noonan. He was wonderfully at home in the world as he never knew it. Despite all kinds of earlier warning signals about what the Japanese had done to our smokestack industries, it was in the Reagan years that they made the critical move against our new high technology industry; our lead in the microchip industry disappeared completely. His indifference to such events seemed not to bother his countrymen. They asked only that he make them feel better, and this he did. He was not an engine of the society but a symptom of it. Poll after poll showed that the American people wholeheartedly believed that personal debt and buying on credit were wrong, yet the uses of credit soared every year. Reagan's was a kind of therapeutic (no-pain) conservatism for the therapeutic (no-pain) society. My favorite story is of Art Buchwald lecturing to a large group of CEOs right after Reagan's second election. "How many here voted for Reagan?" he asked, and virtually every hand in the audience shot up. "And how many here," he continued, "would let him be CEO of your own company?" Not a single hand went up.

The Reagan presidency shows we have done a brilliant job in separating economic realities from the political process. The most interesting question is why this country remains so paralyzed in the face of what would for most countries be threatening news. In 1984 a foreigner visiting America would have thought the country so strong in all respects that the only important issue before us was school prayer; by 1988 the same foreigner must have thought America so shaky a nation in terms of its patriotism that the most important issue before it was the issue of the Pledge of Allegiance.

As I watched the events in Eastern Europe during 1989 (and saw the impact of the American media on these uprisings), I thought that the last great American export is our journalistic freedom and freedom of speech. I remember one particular moment early in the challenge against Ceaucescu in the Romanian uprising, while street fighting was still going on. ABC had managed to interview a citizen in Bucharest who spoke half in tears, half in joy: "We are going to have freedom of speech! A free press! A free mass media! A political system which is pluralistic!" For a moment he seemed almost overcome by his emotions. "The same freedoms you have in the West we are going to have. We are going to be free! Free!"

At a moment when we seem to be teaching much of the rest of the world about the nature of freedom we might well reflect on how we use our own remarkable freedoms. We are more than ever in America an entertainment-driven society. The coming of television has had an overwhelming impact upon individual American institutions and upon our society as a whole. Among other things, television has become our principal means of mass communications. Therefore, we must understand its most important unwritten bylaw: The news must never bore. If we are bored, we will change the channel even though the rest of the world may be doing important things that affect us profoundly. The commercial television system is shaped by its intense drive for ratings and advertising revenues. Ratings, of course, translate directly into the uses of film.

The print media and television have always defined news differently. For a long time insiders have known that with the networks, despite protests to the contrary, a weak story with good film will beat out a good story with weak film. The story of the challenge from Japan reflects this. The resident network correspondents posted there are the invisible men and women of network television. What should be a great story becomes a marginal one. CBS radio in its heyday would have covered it brilliantly; CBS television does it poorly.

The great radio reporters made their reputations as foreign correspondents when America was, like it or not, coming forward to accept its new world responsibilities. There were Murrow and Sevareid in London, Shirer and Smith in Germany, Schoenbrun in Paris, Burdett in Rome. There still remained a certain glory and romance in this, the broadcaster as foreign correspondent, in an age during the war and right after it, when America was reluctantly shedding its isolationist skin. CBS, the best of our radio networks, was then avowedly and openly internationalist, its foreign correspondents our most powerful educators. Today things are different. Being overseas for a network is now by and large considered a detriment to one's career. It has been believed in the post-Vietnam War years that Americans did not want to see foreign reporting or at least wanted to see as little of it as possible. The definition of foreign news steadily changed. Foreign news became important only if (1) something dramatic (and violent) happened to Americans, (2) there was, despite the absence of Americans, truly violent footage, (3) a great spectacle of some sort took place that television would enjoy covering—for example, the coronation of someone in a royal family or the death of an aged leader. The more exotic the spectacle, the better. The current phrase among television producers is "If it bleeds, it leads." Because television news is ever more entertainment-driven, it follows next that its principal people, its anchors, must be stars. In the early days of television, television reporters were not stars. Rather they were modest journalists who more often than not had roots in radio or print and who were trying to master a new professional form, not necessarily with overwhelming success. Their position vis-à-vis their peers was somewhat shaky, and their reputations were based on their personal status rather than on the reputations and power of the organizations they represented. Now the anchor-editor's very presence at the scene of an event guarantees that the story has star quality. Star events merit star coverage.

Inevitably, we in America have become isolated from the realities of the world, and we have come to believe that ordinary nonrevolutionary events overseas have no impact upon us. It has made us more isolationist than we realize. News from Japan does not entertain, as in fact, news from the Communist world, until the populace went into the streets, did not entertain. Predictably, upon the death of Emperor Hirohito, a figure whom the networks had not covered in life, the chance to cover the exotic pageantry of his funeral was irresistible, and it inevitably drew the American anchorpeople to Tokyo.

The parameters of our political system today are derived in no small part by the parameters of our network broadcasting. If the network news trivializes complicated but crucial issues or abdicates from covering them at all, can a trivialized political system be far behind? At the very least what television does is distort a national agenda in favor of a more volatile or confused one based on action or pseudoaction; at its worst it obliterates that agenda. This affects the way we live, the way our political system responds.

Thanks to television, the national agenda becomes not what our long-range or our most pressing problems are, but those that produce the best film. This means that in a mass democratic society, the most critical part of the communications circulatory system—network television—is essentially blocked. As the network news format trivializes political debate, the political system adapts to it. Serious discussion of serious issues is too complicated. Candidates and their advisers learn what the networks want: a telegenic background and a hyped-up attack or counterattack, the more simplistic the better. Television runs only ten- and fifteen-second sound bites from our leading politicians; soon the politicians begin to talk in such brief bites; finally they begin to think in them.

Recently I was on a panel with an anchorman and his executive producer. I mentioned the failure of the networks to cover a story like the economic challenge from Japan (and their attempt to make up for it by using the emperor's funeral as a launch for daily stories on Japan). I pushed even further. Wasn't there a connection between the norms of network television and the growing trivialization of American politics? I asked. Both essentially agreed. The executive producer said it was a serious problem, one the top news executives fought every night. "What we have," he added, "is a conspiracy of a few good men and women" working against that ever-stronger dynamic. I sympathize with him, but it strikes me as a wholly inadequate conspiracy.

Network journalists are constitutionally as free as their print colleagues, but their form is not as free. Form dictates function. If *The New York Times* were to be produced in the format of, say, *USA Today,* filled with factoids, in short, punchy bites, then it would stop being *The New York Times,* not just in form but in substance. Yet our complicated world must fit television's rather uncomplicated format; what is lost is thoughtful civility of discourse.

Television prefers fame to real achievement, and success is determined more and more by television. A journalistic fan of Barbara Walters wrote recently that her specials had replaced *Time* magazine covers as the ultimate symbol of fame. I suppose she was correct, for Walters has developed a shrewd formula: pseudointimate interviews with rock stars or instant celebrities brought to us mostly by some contemporary aberration—Jessica Hahn, Fawn Hall, or Donna Rice. I remember David Riesman, the greatest of American sociologists, on the cover of *Time,* but I do not expect to see him with Barbara Walters.

Unfortunately, other institutions too readily accommodate television's norms. In the late sixties certain authors, because of the success or timeliness of their books, went on television to promote them and became minor celebrities. Very soon the publishing houses turned the process inside out. If writers could become minicelebrities by dint of their appearances on television, why not go to someone who was *already* a celebrity and get him or her to write a book (or lend his or her name to a ghost-written book)? This guaranteed access to the talk shows, but what resulted was a rash of (to be kind) undistinguished books.

If the book publishers understood this kind of media manipulation, so, too, did the members of Congress. If they held a hearing on some important but arcane subject, the networks would not cover it. But if the list of witnesses included Jane Fonda, Meryl Streep, Woody Allen, or, best of all, Cher, the networks could not resist. No one seems to mind that the level of political discourse is the worse for it.

Recently George Kennan, one of our wisest and most articulate authorities on Eastern Europe, spoke on the subject before the Senate Foreign Relations Committee. I watched on television, where his appearance was given some ten seconds, his words paraphrased by the anchorman. Kennan may have prophesied the Cold War more accurately than any other American, his books and memoirs may be national treasures, but clearly, if he is to make himself heard in the new America, he is going to have to learn to be faster and catchier.

For an America less than eager to find fault with itself, Japan, with its trade policies, its legal and cultural protectionism, becomes the perfect foil. If 90 percent of what the Japanese do is easy for us to admire, then it is also comforting to focus on the 10 percent we find so annoying. If there were no Japanese, we would have to invent them. They seem to mock us: hardworking, careful, self-absorbed, utterly devoted to their narrowly defined self-interest. The current economic situation is a dilemma for us both: our economic decline, which our political system has yet to accept; their economic surge, which their political and social systems have not kept pace with.

My view of the struggle between Japan and America keeps changing. When I first went to Tokyo, though I greatly admired how hard the Japanese worked and how much they sacrificed, I was nonetheless irritated by Japan's chauvinism: its innate rejection of almost all things not Japanese, its capacity to slow-walk Americans on issues of trade, its penchant for hiring former high American officials to lobby in Washington, while it denied other nations the right to lobby in Japan—in other words, the failure to understand the concept of reciprocity, that the new international economy is not a one-way street. I was also made uneasy by the extreme sensitivity of the Japanese to any kind of criticism.

Once, early in my first visit, I was asked to speak to a group of important Japanese business executives. Knowing that it was easy to give offense, I spoke carefully for about a half hour, primarily about America's industrial malaise. I praised the efficiency of Japanese workers, and I was extremely admiring of how they had built so much out of so little in so short a time. Then at the very end, very carefully, I offered a few cautionary words about the dangers ahead. I suggested that after so much hard work and sacrifices it would be a shame to damage the relationship between Japan and America because of Japanese protectionism, particularly since if all the barriers were down, the trade deficit would change only about 15 to 20 percent. A lot, I suggested, was being risked for very little. The next day I ran into a friend who was an American consultant in Tokyo. "I hear you gave a Japan-bashing speech yesterday," he said. That was not an atypical story. An American journalist who describes America's fall from grace is regarded as highly intelligent and even courageous; if he brings that same critical eye to Japan's exclusionary trade policies, he is Japan bashing.

One of the least attractive aspects of Japanese nationalism is that it makes visitors equally nationalistic, and unconsciously that happened to me. I do not think it affected my writing or the final quality of my book *The Reckoning,* but it certainly affected the pleasure I took in doing the book. While in fact, it largely praised the qualities that had brought Japan to its industrial excellence, the Japanese, as is their wont with a foreigner, did not make it easy for me. There was a vast instinctive pulling back from my attempts to find things out. In time I grew irritated. Living in Tokyo with my family was expensive. I had no institutional support, all this was coming from my own pocket, and I felt sometimes as if I were running the most expensive taxi meter in the history of mankind. At one point I yelled over the telephone at one of the Nissan public relations men (who was doing a spectacularly successful job in failing to produce the people I needed to see) that he and his company were practicing communications protectionism. I also remember sitting with a top Nissan official who was in charge of quality control and asking him if he could give me an example of a suggestion that came from a quality control circle, was worker-inspired, and had improved the quality of a car. No, he said, he could not. Why not? I asked, thinking this a perfectly legitimate question and envisioning a chapter of the humble young worker who had advanced a brilliant but simple idea that saved his company millions of yen. Because, he said, there were some 36,428* examples of quality control improvements, and he would therefore have to present to me all 36,428 workers responsible for them.

But then I came back to America, and I was beset by a society that was curiously passive about its economic problems. Worse, I saw ordinary citizens unsuccessfully trying to receive minimal acceptable service from fellow Americans; in our modern philosophy of service, the customer is always wrong. I remembered with some nostalgia, not merely the greater efficiency of Japan but the degree to which ordinary people accepted responsibility for what they did. I became churlish about America again. My experience is hardly unique.

I still do not think we as a nation get it. Again and again we look for excuses why the Japanese do things better than we

_____
*I have made up the number here, but the truth is I do not remember whether the number I have made up is larger or smaller than the large number the Nissan official quoted to me.

do. If we are being beaten, then the rules must be wrong; someone must be cheating. Every time we think we have a solution, we are proved wrong. For a long time everyone in Detroit and in many other places believed that the key to Japanese success was the soft yen. So we forced them to reevaluate it and make it harder. They did, suffering a momentary but major shock in their industrial core. For a time their highest executives took major cuts in pay and their work force went on shorter shifts. But because they were process-driven, they soon made their process better. Soon, rather than being the victims of the harder yen, they were its beneficiaries. Their liquidity increased greatly, as ours seemed to decline. American companies and real estate suddenly were for sale at bargain prices. Sometimes it seems to me that the Japanese are so formidable and so supple as competitors that trying to compete with them is like trying to capture mercury. You squeeze it out of one area and it ends up in another. If the yen is harder, they are partially limited as exporters, but they arrive and set up shop as producers in your country as owners, manufacturers, and investors.

Their success, I think, is of a whole; it has no one secret. But let us at least try to understand. For one thing, they continue to want to *make* things. We have turned our energies to other aspects of commerce, aspects that in other times might have been considered ancillary, such as financing and marketing. Making things has a higher social value in their society than ours, I think. Those who run the industrial lines are considered far more important in Japan than they are in America; as a nation they are closer to being the true children of the original Henry Ford than we are. The purpose of their capitalism seems less diluted in contrast with ours. Ours is to make money; theirs is to make products of excellence, which, if they do well, will also, they are sure, make them money.

If there is an equally important part of the Japanese (and

East Asian) success, it is education. The more I think about Japan, the more important education seems to me. Theirs is a very different kind of education from ours, one that many Americans would find unbearable. It emphasizes learning by rote and an acceptance of authority that we consider alien. But even if one dissents from that style of education, one can admire the importance it plays in the society and the respect it inspires in the average Japanese home. A family's position and honor are defined not by how good an athlete a male child is but by how well he does in school. In what was virtually the first interview I did on the subject, I saw Frank Gibney, a prominent journalist-historian. We talked for two hours on a variety of things, but as I was leaving, he turned and said, "Don't forget, education is the stem which winds the watch." The Japanese believe that if they educate their people well, if the educational system works, then all else will take care of itself.

Not long after I arrived in Japan in 1983, I went off to see Michio Nagai, a former minister of education. The interview did not go as I wanted, and it is only now, some seven years after the fact, that I think I understand what he was saying. I asked him about Japanese and American education and education's relationship to the social ethic. Yet he seemed, despite my questions, to want to talk about Korea. The Korean test scores were on the rise, he kept saying, while Japanese scores had been leveling off and actually were even down a little. What does that mean? I asked. Their test scores are a sign that their level of optimism as a society is increasing, and therefore, they will work even harder. Perhaps, he said almost idly, Japan is becoming an old nation already. Its divorce and juvenile delinquency rates are on the rise, he added, not as bad as those in America, but surprising for Japan nevertheless. By contrast, the Korean children still stay home at night to study and listen to their parents. Recently a Korean official had said to him, "'Will

Japan continue to learn the wrong lessons from America or will it start to learn the right lessons from us?" Ten years ago he would never have dared say something like that to a Japanese," Nagai said. "It is a sign that there is a great increase in their confidence." There is a moment, he added, when a society explodes ahead, when its citizens are grateful for the improvement in their lives. Very quickly that balance changes, they become less grateful, and you get the downside of modernization and urbanization. Korea, he said, is just entering that stage, Japan is in the middle of it, and America was on the far side of it. That interview has stayed with me long after it was over.

It makes me think about Winsted, Connecticut. Because my father went back into the service in 1942, my brother and I grew up in a number of cities and towns in America. To the degree that we called a place home it was Winsted, a mill town of about eight thousand in the northwest quadrant of the state. It was something of a melting pot. The largest factory was the Gilbert clockworks, and my generation represented the children and the grandchildren of the immigrants who had worked so hard for so little there. We were to rise above our parents in the ever more just American society.

The school system was, I now realize, excellent. The teachers were Maine schoolmarms—that is, they were women, mostly single, more often than not from tiny farming villages in Maine, where there were no manufacturing jobs. They had come to the great metropolis of Winsted, lured by the prospects of getting at least some peripheral benefit from the Industrial Revolution (the salaries were as high as nine hundred dollars a year; the rare male teacher, of course, always got two hundred dollars more). They were very good. They were fair. They knew a great deal about the uses of authority, having grown up, I suppose, in households where authority was never questioned.

It seems to me that that was a reasonably optimistic time,

even though there was a war on. I think my classmates and their parents believed that the war would one day be over and that our generation was going to have a better life than those who had come before. Parents uncomplainingly made significant sacrifices, and children, without anyone's lecturing them, were aware of those sacrifices. Not everyone in my class had his or her eyes on college—actually those of us who did still represented a minority—but the opportunity was there, and there was a considerable amount of social change in the making. We were, without knowing it, part of a society on the ascent.

That is what Nagai was talking about: a society on the ascent. Japan has been on the ascent since the mid-fifties. It is a nation surging with confidence (and indeed, most recently, for the first time with overconfidence). It does important things right because it does little things right. Japanese good luck is the product of two generations of Japanese making considerable sacrifices to raise their country from the ashes to economic greatness. People's lives in the last twenty and thirty years have gotten better, and while the rate of improvement has slowed down, there is a sense that things are going to get better still. That generates confidence, and confidence generates optimism, which in turn generates social strength. It is a critical factor in the Japanese ascent, and it is one that eludes detection by mathematical formulation. At this point in the cycle people believe that traditional class lines in a society are blurring, and the usual resentments are at least muted. Everyone believes he or she is a part of the new middle class.

Whether Japan can sustain that optimism in succeeding generations when the element of gratitude for hard work may diminish is a critical question for them. Certainly the current generation of Japanese political and industrial leaders is nervous about it. They worry about the ability to sustain success and to sustain the work ethic, and some of their leaders even worry about their educational system and whether or not it is too rigid.

I first met Naohiro Amaya, a high MITI official, in 1983, when I was working on *The Reckoning*. A friend had given me his name, and I was not entirely sure who he was or what I wanted to interview him about. What I found was an historian disguised as a bureaucrat and, more important, a historian who seemed to understand the outline of my book somewhat better than I did. Our first interview was scheduled to last one hour and went on for some two and a half hours. During the nine or so months I worked in Tokyo I went back four more times to talk to him; I felt I had stumbled across a Japanese version of George Kennan, someone with a rare and unusually rich historical perspective through which he saw contemporary events, and because he was Japanese, he saw events through a prism not of West and East but of rich and poor, of those who face adversity and those who come readily upon their riches.

Now he is retired from MITI but still active as an adviser there. He worries constantly about the future. When others in Japan were celebrating the early successes of Japan's new industrial strength, he was already one of those trying to push the economy away from smokestack industries into the new world of high technology, where Japan's educational excellence would be better utilized. In the spring of 1989 I visited with him in Tokyo for two days.

Amaya was bothered by America's failure to adapt to new economic realities. There was not yet a sense of crisis in America, he noted, perhaps because enough people still had some sense of success. As the nation's problems mounted, there was still a tendency to blame others for its difficulties. Perhaps, he thought, it would require some kind of financial shock to jar America out of its complacency, an event on the order of *Sputnik*. He thought that unless America did something to discipline itself, some kind of American monetary crisis was inevitable, because America's financial system was now precariously tied to foreign confidence. Some foreign nation would one day lose its confidence in the American market and then stop buying bonds. That could easily touch off the kind of shock he envisioned.

If there was a coming Japanese crisis, he said, it was likely to be in the area of values and of individual purpose. In some ways Japan's purpose for the last forty or forty-five years had been clear: After the defeat in World War II, it was to catch up with the West. That it had done handsomely, well ahead of schedule. But the question before the nation now was what to do with its new wealth and strength. It was one thing to succeed in an effort to come back from the ashes of defeat; it was another to decide what to do with the benefits. "For forty years we were single-minded in our purpose. We were the greyhound chasing the hare. Now the hare that we chased has disappeared. So who are we and what are we next after the hunt? What is our purpose in life? This is a new question for the Japanese. We are an economic society, and in that period we put aside almost all our political and social issues because we were dealing with things that seemed much more pressing. Now that we have attained economic success we need these other values, and we lack them, and we are not sure how to find them," he said. The easy part was over, he was saying. Were his people prepared to deal with the complexity of their new success, or had they been educated to be merely functionaries of the society?

In the last few years Amaya had become embroiled in a major attempt to reform the Japanese educational system, to have less teaching by rote and a greater emphasis on liberal arts. That had pitted him against powerful, well-entrenched forces in the country's educational lobby. The battle had not gone well. He believed a mistake of historical proportion may have been made as Japan prepared to deal with its future. The nation, he suggested, was producing workers rather than full citizens, and he once told me in passing, almost as a throwaway, that it was a great deal easier to produce a good car than it was to produce a good human being. Was Japan's educational system producing a human being who was essentially a narrow and self-isolating person, and worse, was it producing a person who might soon be functionally obsolete?

That, he said, was the new Japanese dilemma. For the first time the educational system was in danger of doing something wasteful—that is, producing a graduate who was not supple because he or she lacked a broad vision of life. "The problem," he said, "is that we are in danger of producing young people who have the intellectual capacity of computers but who will be inferior to computers in what they can actually do. The computers have caught up. The entrance exam at our universities now is designed to choose students with computerlike capabilities. That means we are geared up to producing people whom we no longer need because the computers will do what they do better than they can do it."

How would Japan deal with the question of wealth? he wondered. Previously that had not been a problem. Now, in the new affluence of Japan's economic success, the young Japanese, like the Americans who had gone before them, were more materialistic. Then he added, "For thousands of years God and poverty kept man disciplined. Now, in the modern age, God is dead and poverty is disappearing. How will we be disciplined?" He was not sure what values the rush to industrialization had left Japan with. How would the Japanese deal with the freedoms and possibilities brought on by a computerized age? "We have just come through an industrial age which ordinary people could easily understand. If we made cars, the average people could understand that and understand the uses of a car. But now we are making computers, and it is not so easy for an ordinary person to make use of a computer. Perhaps for a creative person this will not be a problem, but for others it may be very difficult: What will they do, sit around and use computers to play Nintendo every night? What will be our purpose now?" Perhaps, he said, Japan's great flexibility had been in economic matters and America would turn out to be more flexible in social and political matters.

A book always has a trajectory of its own. It takes you places you did not intend to go and leaves you with thoughts and ideas different from those you had when you began. My book *The Reckoning* began as a book about hardware, about who made better cars, but it became a book about differing social systems and in the end was, somewhat to my surprise, a book about education. After its publication in America, those who were worried about the education gap (instead of the missile gap) seized on it. Because of the book, I became privy to the despair of politicians, businessmen, and finally teachers. I was invited to governors' conferences, regional, national, Republican, and Democratic. The Republican governor of Indiana, wanting to make a major move to upgrade Indiana's schools in his last year of office, used it as the basis of his state of the state speech and gave every member of the legislature a copy. There was among the governors a consensus that we were in a crisis: We do not value education as we once did, our people are essentially indifferent to it, and no one seems to know how to undo that. Almost all the governors have been to Japan and Korea. They have seen the quality of what those countries' educational systems are producing (and how seriously they go at it). When one asks a Japanese company to locate a plant in his or her state, the governor is asked always about the quality of the local schools and the levels of literacy and the young people's ability to read a math manual. Our own businessmen lament the difficulty of getting well-trained people to perform even the most basic skills, skills one always assumed *all* high school graduates had. The bitterest complaints come from our teachers. They often seem defeated by students who will do only the minimum amount of work, who resist homework (as do their parents), and who seem to show a passionate interest in the school only when there is a cutback in athletic or other extracurricular activities. What frustrates them most is that so many of these students come from middle-class homes, and there is an assumption that a college education will eventually follow. "You want to scream at them," a teacher told me one night, "that if they do not work harder, do more homework, meet some standard of knowledge and literacy and use of their own language, they will not be able to go to college, but you would be lying because you know that if they so choose, they can go to a college, and they do. There are enough colleges out there that are run as businesses and need the students and their money now and have brought their standards down to ours, though God knows what these kids will be able to do with their education once they graduate."

The President says that he is an education President, but there is no real sign that he makes a connection between education and the malaise in our economy. That demands a political judgment that he and his predecessor were unwilling to make. Of our various subcultures, only a few (most notably the recently arrived Asian-Americans) see education as the key to the future. Our level of literacy is disappointing compared with other developed nations. We do not really connect education to a better economic life for our children. In the average high school in the average American town, a male child of sixteen who gets good marks, unless he is an outstanding athlete like Bill Bradley, is considered something of a nerd. There are exceptions, of course, the upper-middle-class pockets around the country where people take education seriously, where the excessive price of a house in, say, Scarsdale, or Shaker Heights, or Palo Alto, includes the price of what is virtually a de facto private school education.

Recently I lectured at Hiram College, a very good small private college in Ohio. I spent the evening with a group of bright young people from small towns in the Midwest, representative, I thought, of the core of the country. At one point I asked them to write down on a piece of paper how much homework their high school classmates had done, on the average, each night. Back came the slips. The average figure was thirty minutes. I thought for a moment of Japan and Korea (where children often double-brown-bag it in lower schools because their teachers are graded on how many of their students go on to the next level). I thought of the comparative innocence of my childhood in Winsted, where we thought we were competing for jobs with the students from the even greater metropolis of Torrington, nine miles away. How do you tell today's kids they are competing not merely with the children of a neighboring town, but with the children of Osaka, Seoul, Djakarta, Singapore, Bangkok, and, perhaps soon, Wroclaw, Budapest, and Bratislava?

In 1988 a candidate finally raised the question of the challenge from Asia. The candidate was Dick Gephardt, an ambitious young congressman from Missouri, and the manner in which he raised the question had a familiar ring. The real message was: Once again we were the victims. Gephardt, sensing that the issue was raw, ran as an instant populist, blaming the imbalance of trade entirely upon the Japanese and Koreans. His television commercials, featuring American cars and what they might cost in Asian countries, were intentionally explosive and clearly designed to reinforce jingoistic fear of Asians. There was some small measure of truth to these commercials, but on the whole they scratched the surface of the problem rather than tried to comprehend it. (Gephardt himself knew better, and when he spoke in private, he was far better informed than his commercials implied. He admitted that even if the Japanese opened up their markets, the effect on the trade deficit would not be that substantial.) I watched those commercials, and I envisioned the Gephardt voter: someone who votes no on all school bond issues, doesn't supervise his or her children's schoolwork, and then wonders why the Asians are doing better than we are.

The world moves faster than ever. Change, driven by technology, has a speed of its own. Not to stay abreast is to fall behind. Work demands ever-higher levels of education and competency. That is true not only here but around the world. But as it happens, we are not responding to it. We are hemorrhaging blue-collar jobs, not merely to less developed parts of the world but, as Amaya prophesied, to increasing automation as well. I have a sense of America's changing, of class divisions becoming more sharply defined than at any time since the coming of the New Deal, of a decrease rather than an increase in the forces that work for democracy—not merely political democracy but economic, educational, and social democracy.

So far the changes, the disappointments have not really shown up (or have not shown up too obviously) in our politics; we have been so far spared the politics of disappointment and despair. There are glimpses of it. I was not a great fan of Morton Downey, Jr., and his screaming matches that passed as a talk show, but I thought it was important in that they ventilated some of the deep and abiding anger on the part of Downey's audience against their bosses, their labor leaders, their politicians, their journalists, their system, everyone, it seemed, but Mort himself. The show, and others like it, suggested there is a growing sense of economic disenfranchisement and social bitterness out there. While this frustration has not yet entered mainstream political discussion, one can make the case that covertly it has already altered it, that issues like burning the flag and the Pledge of Allegiance are deft attempts to use it without being caught using it. These are the politics of anxiety and uncertainty rather than the politics of confidence. It will, I suspect, get a good deal worse before it gets better.

The line between those who will be winners and those who will be losers seems sharper than ever, and the line is the product of education. The people at the very top, who go to the best law schools and business schools, become not just winners but big winners. The top law firms and financial houses compete for their services, and each year the starting salaries go higher. A friend tells me it will be eighty-five thousand dollars for a freshly minted lawyer from a top school this year. In the process of seeking such a job, the nature of the verb "to inverview" has changed. When I was young, it meant that you were interviewed, that others who were older and held positions in a given company looked at you as an applicant and judged you on your merits. In the last few years the graduate of a prominent law school *interviews* the law firm—that is, he or she judges the company. Those at the top have too many choices; those at the bottom have too few. The middle class is steadily diminished; the people at the lower end lack the capacity to improve themselves, and those of the upper middle class are motivated by far greater rewards than when I was a boy. As a result the impulse to take care of yourself first and foremost, to use education to seek personal, material rewards rather than to fulfill broader social obligations is ever more powerful. I was never mesmerized by the Kennedy Inaugural speech and the line about asking what you could do for your country instead of what your country could do for you. It always struck me as somewhat hokey, coming from the scion of a family that had just set new records in spending its own personal wealth to place a son in

122

high office. In retrospect, though, the balance between careers in the public and private sectors thirty years ago seems far healthier than today's; a career in the public sector then did not mean immense personal financial sacrifice, as it does now. The Washington I moved to in 1961 was a city in which ordinary people lived with some ease. There seemed to be no rich class, except the tiny handful of people with inherited wealth. That contrasts starkly with today's Washington in which the lobbyists form a new wealthy class and the elected politicians, particularly in the Senate, more often than not have independent means.

Nor is Washington the exception. New York, the city in which I live, is increasingly a city of the rich and the poor, of first and third world populations, the gulf between their worlds ever widening. To the degree that civic virtue exists, particularly among the power elite, it seems propelled by almost reckless selfishness and self-promotion. The contributions of rich families to charities often are minuscule compared to what they spend on gowns and jewelry bought for fund-raising social events.

There are those who still believe that America can move from the strongest core industrial economy in the world to essentially a service economy without losing its greatness, its dynamism, and its industrial health. I am absolutely certain we cannot. I think very few people who go into the service economy will go into what might be called high-service jobs—that is, jobs of value, with leverage and dignity. Far more of them will be jobs in the low-service sector, which require minimal skills and where turnover is constant. Common sense dictates that the healthier the core economy, the healthier the service economy. Nor does it make any sense to believe that the Japanese will automatically deed over to us all financial services necessary to implement the needs of their expanding industrial core. Already seven of the eight largest banks in the world are

Japanese, and while this may be a transitional period in which they need a fair amount of help as they learn to deal with the West, in the long run their need for our financial services will probably diminish.

Slowly and steadily we are creating a new class system, starting at birth, through early education, and finally through colleges and professional and graduate schools. The people on Wall Street who today make such horrendous decisions to close down plants in small towns do it more readily because they have never known the people they are damaging. Because of the way our large companies are structured, there is a lack of accountability at the top as we make endless short-range decisions designed to make the bottom line look better. We will become evermore a nation of social disharmony with a few rich and a great many more poor people who are not only a burden to themselves but a burden on society. That creates a society with distemper, most notably because people have recently lived in greater affluence. This will not be a strong and dynamic America of 250 or 260 million people. In terms of a truly productive society we will be summoning the talents of only 30 or 40 million people. Can that America compete with other powerful nations in the near future?

I am not alone in entertaining such gloomy thoughts. I discussed them recently with Lester Thurow, a prominent economist, a *Newsweek* columnist, and the head of the Sloan School at MIT. "I think it cuts to the core of a question our generation has never faced before: Does America have an establishment or an oligarchy?" he said. "Every day I pick up the newspapers, and journalists describe—and I think they're right—Japan as having an establishment—that is, Japan has a group of people at the very top who may, in fact, be quite as selfish as any other ruling elite of powerful capitalists. But the members of the Japanese establishment know that they and their children cannot succeed, particularly in so small and vulnerable a nation, unless most of the society succeeds as well. So the members of this establishment are willing to sacrifice some of their own personal privilege and power and riches in order to make sure that the larger society works and is regenerative. At the same time, when virtually the same journalists describe Latin American countries, the phrase they invariably use to describe the leadership is the word 'oligarchy.' They are describing a very small handful of immensely privileged people who have it very good and who plan to continue to have it very good and don't care at all about the fact that the rest of the country is doing poorly. In effect, an oligarchy believes it can be successful even if the rest of the country is unsuccessful. Which is why those nations remain so unsuccessful. And that's the system we're moving toward. At different times in this country's history we've had an establishment, and at other times we've had an oligarchy. Right after World War Two we had an establishment which knew we needed something to make Europe healthy because our own health depended on it. So it helped impose the Marshall Plan on an America where great segments of the population were still extremely isolationist and probably did not want it."

An establishment knows it isn't good enough for just its own children to do well, to get on an elite track, because if their own children are running a country where 60 percent of the children cannot make it, something terrible is going to happen.

This situation has been allowed to develop under the veil of America the superpower, the America that could go to the moon and infinitely extend weaponry with dazzling new unusable devices. Now the Cold War is gone, leaving an immense political, economic, and psychological gap in our lives. Will we be nostalgic for its simplicity, for the easy divisions between East and West, for its rhetoric from both sides that came so readily?

We now live in a world where the tensions are more likely to be North-South, white-nonwhite, rich-poor, developed-underdeveloped, educated-uneducated. We grew up fearing the power of a strong Russia; how then do we adjust to a world in which a greater threat to our stability comes from a weak Mexico? The Cold War inevitably perverted the nature and the purpose of our society. We went in the beginning from identifying and meeting a real threat with measures that were legitimate to creating, almost without knowing it, a dominating national security infrastructure with a dynamic and a life of its own. Our federal educational bill and our national highway bill of the fifties, as my friend Martin Nolan of the *Boston Globe* likes to remind me, are the National Defense Education Bill and the National Defense Highway Bill. The first major computer produced by IBM was called, for patriotic reasons (and to bring along recalcitrant factions within the company), the Defense Calculator. Such labels were more prophetic than anyone realized; we were, over many years, first and foremost a national security state in a time of peace. That became our governing obsession.

Standing in Red Square in 1990, I could suddenly see Russia for what it was, a sluggish society with a great many missiles and not much else. Now we must look at our own shortcomings and judge ourselves not by the standards of competition with the Soviets but by the norms of a harmonious and decent society. Finally, after all these years, the face in the mirror is our own.

Epilogue One:
Iraq

AFTER IRAQ UNDER SADDAM HUSSEIN crossed the border in August 1990 and invaded Kuwait, George Bush moved quickly and systematically to take action. He assembled a multinational force of some 500,000 men and women, primarily American, and ringed the Iraqi forces. While an anxious nation watched, transfixed in its living rooms over several months, the two-stage war unfolded; the first stage seemed to those at home, a kind of video war, one of high technology, the ultimate in the wired world, in which Americans could sit and watch on their television screens Pentagon film of the use of our high technology against Iraq (it was not, the commanding general there, General Norman Schwarzkopf, noted angrily, a game of Nintendo); the second of it came eventually when the ground war was launched, and lasted four days. That second part, because of Vietnam, was preceded by considerable trepidation.

Saddam's army had struck quickly against Kuwait with devastating quickness and success. Then it had begun the long parched wait in the sun for the approaching mechanized armada of the hated infidels from the West, the Americans. Of the outcome, for most Western observers, there could be no doubt. Of what the price would be there was great doubt—whether the Americans would be forced to take immense casualties; 10,000 or 20,000 young Americans killed so far from home in a war, where even as they waited for battle to begin, their ally, the Saudis, would not permit them to drink a beer or pray to their god. (I thought that if the Americans could conclude the ground war with 3,500 or fewer casualties they would be lucky; the figure of 5,000 struck me as in the high range. For the record, the American military ordered 16,000 body bags sent to Desert Storm.)

In addition there was a secondary factor—how long would the war be fought? A quick dramatic war with successful use of modern technology favored the Americans. A longer war, one of several months in which Saddam could hold out against the infidels, might show that he was even in defeat worthy of being the great leader of all the Muslim world, a military defeat from which might accrue great political benefits. Saddam himself had believed the casualties would be too high for the Americans, that he could tie them up in a prolonged desert war, and that they, a spoiled Western nation fighting so far from home, would turn against the war. He had boasted of this, that what had happened in Vietnam would now happen in the desert. But the desert was not likely to be another Vietnam. It was, above all, an open area, well suited to the use of modern technology, and even a desert war in which his troops fought well might be over very quickly. It would be very different from Vietnam, which lasted some ten years for the Americans. But clearly that was what Saddam was hoping for. He had boasted to the American ambassador and others, long before America became involved, that Americans were a soft people who would have no stomach for a long war, taking place so far away, and that they would not be able to bear 10,000 casualties.

In the days before and after America's quick victory there was a great deal of discussion about what became known as the Vietnam Syndrome, a phrase never particularly well defined—it could mean many different things to many different people—but apparently was best interpreted as meaning that the Vietnam experience had been so traumatic that America would never use its military power again, particularly in a distant war against an underdeveloped nation. It turned out that no one was suffering so severely from the Vietnam Syndrome as Saddam Hussein. He completely misread the difference between war in the jungle and war in the desert.

The differences between the wars in Iraq and Vietnam were fairly obvious even before the stunningly quick American victory. In Vietnam, America fought a political war, self-evidently on the wrong side, trying to suppress a revolution against colonialism and neocolonialism which had already been going on for almost twenty years when the first Amercian ground troops were sent in. For every Vietcong or NVA soldier killed by the Americans there was always someone else to take his place, a son or a nephew. For the Americans this had clearly been the wrong war in the wrong place at the wrong time. Although America held absolute military superiority—the Vietcong and NVA held absolute *political* superiority. That is, no matter how many Vietnamese the Americans killed, the next day their sons, nephews and brothers would join up and continue the fight. We were in effect fighting the birthrate of the nation. We could fight well and kill, but nothing grew underneath our military shield.

In addition, our vaunted military technology was never applicable in Vietnam; it was diluted and weakened by the force of two things—the capacity of the NVA to fight at night, which greatly diminished our technological edge, and it was diminished as well by the extraordinary terrain and the thick foliage of the countryside, which allowed vast armies to move around undetected by Western eyes. The Vietminh had also learned a critical lesson very early in the war. By the time the Americans arrived the NVA had already defeated first the French and then the South Vietnamese. So when the first American units—the elite of a formidable army—arrived, the NVA decided to study how to neutralize the Americans. Given the immense American technological superiority, they needed to find a way to stand up to the Americans. They found it very quickly. They decided that the way to neutralize the overwhelming American advantage in weaponry—the jet fighter bombers, the armed helicopters, the artillery pieces and armored vehicles which were airlifted in to battles—was to close to within thirty meters. Most armies in the past had done their basic infantry killing at some one hundred to two hundred meters. This war was to be different. If the Americans wanted to call in air strikes, let them in effect call them on their own troops as well.

By contrast, Saddam Hussein was not in the process of fighting a revolutionary war. (And the Americans were very careful not to occupy Iraq after their victory. If they had, the war might have become very different; every Iraqi citizen might have become a potential terrorist and once again we would have become bogged down, not unlike the French in Algeria.) He proclaimed himself a revolutionary but much of the revolution was about consolidating his own mounting personal power. On the way to taking power he had defeated no French 'or British colonial army. He might be seen throughout much of the Muslim world as a Muslim leader, but in fact he had come to power after the colonial powers had left. His army was not a guerrilla army, it had fought in no great national cause, it was in fact very much a conventional force and very much like the armies which America had fought with the greatest measure of success in this century. It was dependent upon traditional battle formations, it used tanks, airpower, and artillery to crush foes. Thus it offered, in sharp contrast to the NVA, marvelous and very tangible targets for the vastly superior American technological arm. A phrase eventually used in the briefings during the Persian Gulf War was an interesting one: the briefers spoke of a particular area still being "target rich." Target rich! That was never a phrase used in Vietnam briefings. The enemy there struck at night and disappeared during the daytime. In Vietnam, the one-cell nature of the war, the fact that the average NVA infantryman used his legs rather than mechanized vehicles (and could go twenty miles at night over very difficult terrain carrying only a basic weapon, a limited amount of extra ammunition, and a few days of rice and the fish sauce, *nuoc mam*), meant that the other side never gave America a target. We were in the business, one frustrated pilot told me, of making toothpicks there, and of blowing up the same bridges and bicycle factories and forests every day.

Iraq was to be very different, and the American command knew it from day one—if for no other reason that Saddam's army was an Oil Century force, highly mechanized, with billions invested in its tanks, helicopters, planes and artillery pieces. It was an awesome force against those who, like the poor Kuwaitis, had less in the way of equipment, but vulnerable to those who are more modern, who had in fact graduated from the Oil Century club of mechanized warfare to the newest and most exclusive club, the computer-laser club.

Saddam's force was deployed in the desert, highly visible even when camouflaged, vulnerable to the most scathing and relentless and unsentimental modern photo reconnaissance in the history of mankind— for the men and women who read the satellite photo printouts are the secret wizards of this war, comparable to the codebreakers on World War II. (Winston Churchill, at the end of World War II, had referred to the arrival of the new technology of rockets and radar as the coming of "the wizard war.") What no one knew yet was that, in the Persian Gulf, the world was going to see the deployment of the first great force of the wizard military against an Army whose essential roots were still in World War II. We knew where they were, we knew who they were, and, as one American commander told a friend of mine, we even knew how many times a day their commanders went to the bathroom.

On the surface Saddam's weaponry seemed extremely modern; that is, he had helped himself to what was virtually the most modern of Soviet and French planes, tanks, and missiles, and he had, it appeared from intelligence reports, even improved and modernized some of the weapons he had bought from the European nations. The knowledge that, with the help of a rogue Canadian inventor, he had been trying to develop a new super artillery piece, the biggest gun in the world that was based on designs left over from World War I, but modernized and perhaps even more terrifying, retooled to include a capacity for firing chemical and biological shells at enemy armies, was ominous of itself. It left those who scrutinized him with an eerie feeling that he was pushing his weaponry ahead of even the most developed industrialized nations. The skill with which the component parts for his super gun and for his gasworks were illegally laundered in Western Europe was troubling as well. If his army was not one to threaten the two or three Superpowers, it was nonetheless on the verge of becoming a devastating regional force, so much greater, and richer, and larger than any comparable army in the region that the balance of power in the world might shift. If Saddam had conquered Kuwait successfully, he might have been able to dictate oil prices even to those states which profoundly hated him, like the Saudis. He would not even have needed to invade Saudi Arabia—just taking the Kuwaiti oil money, building his force into an ever greater regional army, he would have cast so large a shadow on the Saudis that they, rich under the ground, weak in all other things, would have had to accede to his will on oil pricing.

No one, of course, knew how good the Iraqi army really was. It had fought both well and badly during the eight year war with Iran, a war which had gone virtually unreported in the developed world. It had fought reasonably well in defense and poorly on offense (as, more often than not, had the Iranians). This is not unusual in the underdeveloped world; even poor troops who are poorly led will fight well in defense of their homeland. To fight well on offense is an entirely different story. It demands not merely a large and well-armed force, but a coherent, well-led one as well; a modern not a feudal command structure; a sense of motivation and discipline which is exceptionally high; and the capacity not merely to own modern weapons like jet planes, but to use them as well.

In most of the previous wars in the Middle East, in which the Israelis had so successfully smashed and humiliated the varying Arab forces arrayed against them, the difference was rarely one of military budget, nor was it the size of the respective Armies (the Israelis were always outnumbered); rather it was that the Israelis were the prototype of the new modern state in both social *and* military terms. In

Israel the military was merely an extension of civilian and social strength and purpose. It was well led from top to bottom, and the Israeli military structure reflected the country's political and social structure. Command was always granted on the basis of military ability alone and never on the basis of political connection or cronyism. The Arab army structure, by contrast, was more often than not a reflection of a feudal society, or of a society struggling to move from a postcolonial, feudal incarnation to a modern one. Typically, in past wars, the Israelis had struck quickly and with strength, and Arab troops, often as well armed, used their modern equipment poorly. They were often poorly led (their commanders as often as not held their commands based on political connections rather than ability), and they refused to fight at night—even their pilots sometimes would not fly in the dark.

In fact, watching the 1967 Six-Day War in the Middle East where the Israelis, so greatly outnumbered, made such quick work of all the varying attacking Arab forces, I was struck—I was still a reporter in Vietnam at the time—by the similarity between the Israelis and the North Vietnamese. Both societies, despite their ideological differences, had dynamics which had forced them to modernize. The North Vietnamese had become modern because they needed the best talent of a generation to throw off first the French and then the Americans; and the Israelis, poised ever on the very edge of survival, a tiny nation surrounded by enemies, could not afford the luxury of a corrupt chain of command. (The one organization in all of Israel which has dared not be governed by anything other than meritocratic procedures, is the Israeli Air Force.) The Arab nations in conflict with Israel were mired in terms of social, political, and cultural practices from their deeply unhappy feudal past. Having modern equipment to draw oil from the ground, having modern technicians around your country rigging up modern satellite stations, and even having enough money to buy the world's most modern jet fighters does not make you modern.

This then was the critical question which lingered in the weeks and months after Saddam Hussein had scored his first stunning victory against Kuwait: how modern was his army? For having modern equipment was one thing, but using it in a modern and effective way was another. To have a modern army he needed modern commanders, and modern commanders are likely to be talented and brave and create their own cults—they might become popular and if they were popular they would become a threat to *him*, leader of all leaders. Was Saddam's human command structure modern enough for his jet fighters, his missiles, and his new tanks? No one knew the answer but there was reason to doubt it. For, whatever strengths the Iraqis had shown during the Iranian war, they had also shown themselves weak in logistics, weak in using their airpower effectively (their pilots tended to eschew the type of close level support that their planes were designed for and to bomb from much too high an altitude, making the Air Force virtually useless), and their command structure seemed to be riddled with favoritism. There had been moments during the Iranian war when, facing a terrible defeat at the hands of the Iranians, talented men had been promoted and had led the Iraqi troops well, but when things had returned to normalcy they were said to have died in most unfortunate accidents. All of this was important because it is one thing to buy modern technology and it is quite another thing to use it well. If Vietnam was a war in which America fought a modern foe armed with primitive weapons, then the Persian Gulf was the opposite—one in which we fought a politically primitive foe armed with modern weapons.

The American weaponry itself by contrast was staggering. In Vietnam much of America's weaponry had been inapplicable, and some of it was not particularly good. (It was one of the shames of that war, that the basic infantry weapon of the more primitive opponent, the AK 47, was considered by the average grunt to be a better weapon than the American new NATO rifle which was prone to jam in the tropical setting.) This time it was different. Everything worked. No one had known how good the Abrams tank would be and it turned out to be very good indeed, roaring across rough desert terrain at thirty miles an hour, going up and down valleys, while its gun, because it was gyro supported, always even and focused, never off the target. These tanks had the capacity to roar across the desert, spot the enemy tanks, measure quite exactly the distance between them, and, if they were still within range of the enemy, back up slightly until they had a monopoly on battlefield range and then blast away. The technology of twenty-five years of computers and lasers grafted on to modern weaponry was unbelievably effective. In the end it was a war fought with few battles, what the Americans call a done deal from the beginning. No one, not even the most optimistic of American commanders, had thought the principal problem once the ground war began would be that of handling the thousands and thousands of prisoners, or that the Americans during the ground fighting would lose fewer than one hundred men. It was the rarest of wars, one in which air power completely crushed a land-based force.

In the end, the principal memory is of the main highway littered with the carcasses of Iraqi tanks escaping from Kuwait, heading back home, swift but not swift enough. When the American ground troops finally reached the wreckage of vehicles on the Kuwait-Basra highway, where the Warthogs and other planes had destroyed the Iraqi armor, they found the hulls of modern armored vehicles along with stolen Mercedes and BMWs, and stolen television sets. The conquerors of Kuwait had died in the ignominy of fleeing the city, burdened primarily by their shame and their loot. In some four days the war was done. Only the policing up remained. The most memorable film clips from the war were not of battle—for the battle was generally over before the cameras arrived—but of the long lines of Iraqi soldiers outlined against the desert, hands over their heads, surrendering, an image seen with great relief in the West, but in the Arab world, the remembrance of another great humiliation vested upon the Muslim world by the infidels from the West.

The war had lasted four days, no one had dared belive that so vast a force could undertake so difficult a task so far away with so few casualties. For a brief moment there was a kind of national euphoria. The euphoria did not last long. It never does. For a brief period, a very brief period indeed, there was an unreal feeling in America, a kind of national emotional high. Everyone felt better about him or herself. It had all seemed so swift and easy. Saturday Night Live, the popular comedy show, put on a satirical advertisement on an Iraqi version of G.I. Joe. Iraqi Joe the new doll was guaranteed to bend down and kneel and surrender to other toys.

Never in the post war years had a president stood so high in the polls. The Democratic opposition seemed to shrivel up. When the president addressed the joint session of the Congress it seemed less a scene from a democratic society than one from a monarchy, or a coronation, with members of both parties pushing and shoving to get close to him and pay court. Congressman Newton Gingrich, a hawkish Republican conservative who has never heard a shot fired in battle suggested that all the Democrats who voted against the president's decision to go to war should publicly apologize—a sort of national moment of atonement for the opposition party. That it was the president's victory, political as well as military, there was no doubt. He had been the most committed of hawks, more committed from the start than those around him to go to war and make Saddam Hussein pay for his aggression. Many members of the bureaucracy were lukewarm toward the idea; two former chairmen of the Joint Chiefs of Staff argued against military intervention and for sanctions, as did some seven former Secretaries of Defense. The president himself, who had never felt particularly popular—it was Ronald Reagan who was always popular and George Bush who had stood for so long in his shadow,(as he had stood in the shadow of other Republicans before Reagan, Nixon and then Ford)—seemed to glory in his moment in the sun. The popularity was his own, hard won and not derivative, and not handed down by an exceedingly popular predecessor. The Wimp Syndrome was apparently finally over, and the idea that the president was not manly enough. It is part of the irony of American politics that the public at large had judged Ronald

Reagan, who had barely deigned to serve his country during World War II (his service entailed living in Hollywood and donning a uniform several days a week in order to make propaganda movies— not the riskiest of roles), based on the ease with which he walked and the ease with which he uttered challenging words, to be tough and worthy and George Bush, who had in fact a quite distinguished war record, the youngest naval pilot in the war, was judged more harshly largely by dint of manner, body language, and most of all, a somewhat unfortunate capacity to sound shrill on important occasions. If American politics were viewed as a movie, which it increasingly seems to be, it would be Ronald Reagan who would ride in at the last minute, utter the fewest number of words, and thus get rid of the bad guys and save the girl; George Bush would have been cast as an urban anti-hero in a comedy about a decent young man who does not do well in his particular profession, is a bit of a bumbler, fails to live up to the exacting standards of a strong mother, is largely protected in his career by a strong wife, and whose fantasy, as he bumbles through his office chores, is to be a hero of the old cowboy West. Reagan, hero of all those endless Hollywood movies, had an easy, almost careless, virile style, and he was a man that other men liked and judged to be a role model. The vice-president, born and bred to a proper upper-class family in the eastern establishment, the best of our elite, schooled at Andover, Yale, who made a mid-career move to Texas, always seemed caught between his two personas. Was he the upper-class son of the East, or the new rough-and-ready oilman of the West? (He was, the former Texas governor and rancher, John Connally, once noted in a devastating putdown, as a rancher, all hat and no cattle—that is he owned the hat and the clothes to look like a Westerner, but that was as far as it went. There were no cattle and there was no ranch.)

Finally with the overwhelming victory of American forces in the Persian Gulf, Bush seemed free of the past, liberated at last and a considerable figure in his own right (although not as big a hero as General Schwarzkopf who has been offered, it is said, some

$5 million for the world rights to his memoirs, which would put the value of his experience in the Persian Gulf at roughly $1.25 million a day for the ground fighting). But Bush needed no great book royalties, the psychic reward was great enough, he seemed free of the burden of the past and the shadow of Reagan.

The great question, as the president surveyed this exceptional victory, was what he was going to do with the accrued popularity and political leverage, for rarely in the last thirty years has an American president loomed so large on the landscape and seemed able to dictate an agenda. He had certainly invested none of his popularity in the preparation for the war. The chance to use the sending of the vast American force and air armada as a rationale for finally bringing the price of gas up to world reality (it is one fifth at the pump of that charged in most developed countries), and using the extra money not merely to apply against the budget deficit, but to discipline Americans against the pressures of the Arabs, did not appeal to him. He added five cents to the tax. The question remained, What would his post-war agenda be—to which of America's pressing problems would he devote his considerable leverage? Delighting in this moment of glory the president announced that the Vietnam Syndrome was finally over and that he and the American forces in the field had put it to rest. To some that seemed an odd theme, indeed a potentially danger- ous one. Did this mean that America, for a time involuntarily tempered by battlefield defeat, might not edge once again towards a kind of arrogance of power, that it would consider any place on the globe a safe target for American interventionism, despite the local political realities? Was there to be in the wake of this exceptional victory a *Pax Americana* which would make another Vietnam possible?

Those of us who never thought that there was a Vietnam Syn- drome were puzzled by his statement. We never thought America had been in palpable military terms weak during or after the Vietnam War, and we thought that we were no stronger after the Persian Gulf War than we had been before it. What was true in fact was not so much that America was stronger or weaker after the Persian Gulf

War, but that a great many Americans felt better about their country's strength, and therefore felt at least momentarily better about themselves and their lives. That is not, however, the kind of glow which lasts a long time. In America every year there is a penultimate championship professional football game, called the Super Bowl, and it is true that when a particular team wins, the fans of that team and the residents of its city feel (momentarily at least) much better about themselves. For a brief time these people, who do not like their jobs very much, forget that they do not like their bosses, and those whose marriages are marked by bitter strife, forget their domestic discord. Blacks and whites are said to get on better because the stars of the team are usually both black and white. This usually lasts for three or four days, a week at the most. It is arguable that for the players and the coaches, that is, the actual participants who have sacrificed so much for so long and who have often been working towards this goal for their entire careers, the good feeling lasts a long time.

Winning the Persian Gulf War was, I suspect, for most Americans, very much like winning a kind of national Super Bowl and every city and town in the country not only felt that it had won, but that America had at last avenged the frustrations of Vietnam, and the humiliations and indignities inflicted by the Ayatollah. For a very brief time the entire country felt very good about itself, and then because it all happened so quickly, and because so very few families had actually participated, that is, had sent sons or daughters to the Gulf, the good feeling dissipated with equal speed. After all, even as a war, it was to an uncommon degree a spectator sport. We had, most of us, watched rather than participated. Our participation extended largely to sitting in front of a television set, holding a control module and switching from one network to another to see which one had the best footage or the most interesting guest commentator on the war.

The air war had been very exciting in the beginning, seemingly bloodless, at least on the allied side, and one sided, with amazing footage showing the accuracy of the new laser-guided bombs, and then when the ground war had finally begun, it had taken place virtually without opposition—four quick days of unparalleled and devastating technological might against an exhausted and finally defeated army. The ground war had turned out to be not so much a ground war as people had expected, but rather an extension of the air war, almost all of the killing done air to ground.

So the Persian Gulf war had come and gone so quickly that it had left us with very few memories, no prolonged battles for a key city to enthrall us. As it had been brief and few of us had participated, and by and large none of us had sacrificed anything, we were left primarily with a feeling of emptiness. Six months later few Americans could remember the name of any single battle, because there were in fact almost no battles. There had been no rationing, no increase in the price of gas to bring it to market value, no draft of our young men and women.

For a time the most serious debate had been not so much about whether or not to fight the Iraqis, but whether we were violating our domestic constitutional traditions of free journalism and whether the Pentagon was controlling the news media to too great a degree. For most Americans watched the war on television and, if we truly wanted to feel patriotic (or at least be perceived by our coworkers and neighbors as patriots), we went down to a local store and bought a yellow ribbon to put outside our houses and a small flag or ribbon to place in our lapel. There was an enormous orchestrated feeling of patriotism during the war, but it was largely artificial, orchestrated by the government and the great media centers like Hollywood and New York. The contrast between this and the more genuine patriotism of World War II, when the entire country was involved, is breathtaking. In World War II, the war lasted some four years and almost every American home made some kind of dramatic sacrifice, and the entire country *participated*. In that war almost everyone who was able-bodied served. There was a draft; it was deemed equitable and democratic. There was rationing and you did not put a flag in your window unless you either had a son in the service or one who had been killed in action. By contrast the Persian Gulf was the most vicarious of wars, and if that was the good part it was also the bad part—most of the country was properly distanced from events. It was good in theory if not in practice.

I had a considerable number of conversations during those weeks with friends and acquaintances who would say that they were for the war, that something had to be done about Saddam. What about your own son? I would on occasion ask, mentioning a male child of twenty-one or twenty-two in my colleague's family. "Oh I don't mean for *him* to go," the answer would inevitably come back, "but we have this good new professional army and they can go." More than in wars past, this was one in which the elite of the country agreed that there was something worth doing but that it should be done by other people's children.

As most of us made no sacrifice during the war we had no permanent feeling when it was over. Our lives were much the same when it was over. A number of television stations and newspapers did programs and ran long articles questioning whether the same age of prosperity and good feeling which had followed the end of World War II would take place now. After all we had fought well and successfully in World War II; it had gone largely according to plan, and when it was over, there had been a carryover effect into peacetime and we had entered a period of unparalleled prosperity, a period only now just ending. Didn't it follow, they seemed to be asking, that since the Persian Gulf War was such a success, we would again feel good about ourselves and that there would be a similar carryover effect from the war into our domestic politics?

That the differences between the two periods was immense seemed beyond the limited historical grasp of the reporters. Not only was there a quantum difference in national participation at that moment forty-six years ago, but the war had brought America, until then a sleepy and essentially isolationist nation, kicking and screaming to the zenith of its power and to a new and not entirely comfortable international role. It was mighty and young and optimistic in a world that had been twice ravaged by war within twenty years and that was poor and in rubble and pessimistic. The America which had emerged from World War II was aptly described by the British historian Robert Payne in 1949:

"There never was a country more fabulous than America. She sits bestride the world like a Colossus; no other power at any time in the world's history has possessed so varied or so great an influence on other nations . . . Half the wealth of the world, more than half the productivity, nearly two thirds of the world's machines are concentrated in American hands; the rest of the world lies in the shadow of American industry, and with every day the shadow looms larger . . ."

That, of course, is the main difference between America today and America forty-six years ago. The America revealed at the end of the Persian Gulf War is, for all of that quick and handsome victory, a nation filled with self-doubt, unsure of itself, and still living over its head. Unable to discipline itself, it remains a debtor nation. Its trade balance with the rest of the world is badly skewered, while its financial system is still dependent upon others, principally the Japanese and the Germans, to buy its treasury bonds. Its banking system, because of immense debt loaded on by the manipulators in the 1980s, is shakier than at any time in the last fifty years. Even its children's test scores are down. There is considerable doubt about America's ability to compete industrially with other nations. The relationship with the Japanese, which is so crucial to the domestic economy, grows edgier and edgier on both sides and seems to remain very much on the back burner for the current administration. An American expert on Japan in September, 1991 noted that there were two countries in the world that Secretary of State James Baker does not visit, his own, and Japan. The so-called financial heroes of the 1980s, the men who made millions, indeed billions, leveraging their fortunes often with the use of junk bonds, have ended up in prison or, at the very least, seen their fortunes collapse and been forced to sell their companies (more often than not to European or Japanese buyers because American buyers lack the cash).

In the Reagan era, an era in America where there was a *quid pro quo*, the ordinary people who voted for Ronald Reagan agreed to accept him at face value and not to scrutinize him too closely with regard to his political and economic activities; even if the decisions he made were clearly unsound, as long as he made them, he made his voters feel better, at least momentarily, about themselves. That America in those years had no right to feel good about itself—those were the years in which the budget deficit and trade deficit mounted at appalling rates—was beyond the point. It was that very ability to permit the country to have an era of good feeling even though every serious economic sign was a disaster that was so attractive about Reagan.

That particular honeymoon is now over; if anything, there are a growing number of Americans who have turned very bitterly on Reagan, as if finally waking up to the evidence that had been in front of them for a decade. Nothing has declined more rapidly in recent American political life than Ronald Reagan's reputation; indeed, a somewhat trashy book by a gossip writer named Kitty Kelley, describing the seedy underside of the Reagans' personal lives, has become oddly enough not so much what one would have expected—a mere juicy bit of semi-salacious gossipy reading—but a major political statement. It is a *cause célèbre*, and in bookstores people have actually lined up to buy it. It is as if there is a dual judgment going on here: Ronald and Nancy Reagan held themselves up as custodians of the best of American values, *family* values which Americans fear are in serious decline these days, and the nation so accepted them. Now it turns out that not only were their politics something of a sham—sham conservatism—but their personal lifestyles were not a reflection of the wholesome, God-fearing America that they proclaimed, they were above all as a family about as incompetent and unloving a unit as one can imagine. (Perhaps the most devastating story in the Kelley book is the story of Nancy Reagan using the Secret Service, a force entailed to protect the President and his family, to spy on her children and report back on them. Not surprisingly the children, finding out that they were being spied on, got rid of their Secret Service details.) The Reagans professed to raise the moral tone of American life, and in fact lived quite different lives. They were in reality exactly what they condemned, and I suspect this is the reason for the absolutely astonishing success of Miss Kelley's book and why its success is something of a political event. Five years ago the same book might not have sold very well, and at the very least it would have been violently assaulted by defenders of the president and his wife; now, not only is it selling at a record rate, but the former president has remarkably few defenders. It is as if what the Reagans stood for in theory and what they did in practice symbolized the 1980s, a decade already in great disrepute in America. In effect, America got what it wanted with the Reagans, a chance to evade dealing with its real problems for almost a decade while living over its head, and still having the ability to feel good about itself. It was perceived as a good deal while it lasted, but the deal seems to be over.

Elsewhere in the Middle East there may be less change than most people suspect. The United States has been brought in as a direct player in the region as it has never been before. The leverage of the United States on varying Arab countries has so far proven debatable. Old and bitter hatreds, grievances of the centuries, do not change because one small-time tyrant momentarily overplayed his hand in the desert. American military power has the capacity to destroy a tyrant, but it lacks the force to make so angry a region bend to its will.

The Alliance which fought Saddam Hussein was put together out of many parts, and many allies, such as the United States and Syria were the most unlikely of bedfellows. What held it together was a sense of the negative, the bond of countries which hated Saddam for very different reasons—the Americans under Bush because of what he was; the Syrians under Assad, because they probably envied him what he was doing and would have been glad to have done something comparable. With Saddam diminished, the glue which held it together is largely gone. Probably the amazing thing about the Alliance is that it held together as well as it did; but it was certainly an uneasy force where no one would have wanted to know what their partners were saying about them in private. Even as the war was over, the Americans found themselves immensely irritated with their chief ally, the Emir of Kuwait, finding that it was unusually difficult to get him to return to his country, and the American people were more than a little miffed to find that in a time of terrible destruction and great hardship, a number of American engineering units were immediately ordered to repair the emir's palace first and foremost. That was not exactly surprising, emirs tend to be like that, as indeed shahs are like that, but it did not help the feeling on the part of ordinary Americans that they had just completed a war for a better and more egalitarian world.

Now that the war is over, of course peace becomes the more difficult issue. The truth is that the Americans are trying to sell a peace process for the region, a plan which suits their needs, but they are already finding that among many of their instant allies, it was easier to sell something negative like stopping Saddam Hussein than something positive like a regional peace plan. Their efforts, therefore, are so far fragile.

The differences between the varying Arab countries, as well as the Arab antagonism with Israel seem as great ever. America's connection to its new allies is at best tenuous; even as the Kuwaitis were being overrun by the Iraqis, they were reluctant to ask for American help, indeed the Iraqi troops were practically inside the palace before they did. The Saudis were not very different. Fearing their vulnerability and their isolation as a rich feudal monarchy in a region ripe for anti-monarchist and radical political movements, they have needed American military aid against their hostile neighbors but they have always been wary of asking American troops to come, for fear of being seen too openly as the protegé of the infidels. Reluctantly in the end they asked for help, and they got it, and with that a bridge was erected, probably with a certain finality. That which had always been true, Saudi dependence upon American military power, was now out in the open.

In the immediate sweetness of the victory there was much discussion in the United States about who were the winners and who were the losers, and there was much discussion that both the Jordanians, because of King Hussein's unfortunate decision to favor Saddam (and quite deliberately stick his finger in the eye of the United States), and the PLO were the major losers. But the truth is that the king is not much diminished because there is not much to diminish. He is what he has always been, a survivor, loved and respected by few, vulnerable to the surrounding powerful and radical forces. It is the judgment of the American government and a few of its allies that he is the lesser of several potential evils, and so he is kept in power, as much as anything else, by the tolerance and forbearance of two nations which he publicly scorns, the United States and Israel. It is part of the ongoing charade about the king that he is allowed to give speeches which ring with Arab nationalism, and he is allowed to scorn his protectors, while they in turn pay little attention to his speeches and accept him for what he is—in their eyes, the best of a bad lot.

As for the PLO, it remains the PLO; it favored Saddam, which was no surprise, its adherents cheered as SCUD missiles flew overhead and hit Israel. Technically therefore it is a loser. Yet as it loses, so does everyone else. It does not go away. The plight of the Palestinians, the tensions between Arab and Jew over the West Bank remain the implacable problem of the Middle East. Nothing else can be settled as long as the Palestinian Question is not settled. Thus if the Palestinians, in their desperation and their pathetic decisions to cheer for Saddam are losers, then everyone else in the region suffers as well; it is a region where the victors are always impaled on the problems, and indeed the anger and hostility of the losers.

In the meantime the region rearms. It remains the tinderbox of the world, countries too rich and too angry for their own good. The long hard arduous road to the creation of a decent harmonious state, one in which a country invests in the long haul for education, housing, and industry is difficult and the rewards are always in the future; the results are difficult to perceive and indeed often threatening to the more far-sighted of tyrants. The easy and quicker road to glory is to buy arms. Out of this comes instant majesty and instant reputation. In terms of an atomic balance in the region, the destruction of Saddam's nuclear capacity means that of all the countries in the region only Israel has a nuclear capability. That does not mean that others will not try to become members of the nuclear club. As long as the Israelis have the bomb, the Arabs will seek it, and as long as they have as much money as they do, thanks to the oil, there will be an arms race.

What was interesting about the Persian Gulf War was that it showed that the level of weaponry—the result of some twenty-five years of a regional arms race—has come ever closer to the atomic level itself, dangerously close. There is less and less of a buffer zone between the level of weaponry and rocketry achieved in this war, and the atomic ceiling just above it. What is clear in this region is that each year starting with the Six Day War in 1967, when the Egyptians launched with no great effectiveness a number of anti-aircraft missiles at Israeli planes, the level of weaponry has escalated at a terrible rate. The distances beween the countries has not grown any greater, and the missiles themselves have gotten ever faster and more powerful. If laser and computer guided missiles are the American weapons of today, how long before they become the property of the client states in the region? The cost, after all, is not a problem, and there is no reason to believe that of the many powerful states developing weapons at this level, there is not at least one which will sell them to some Arab country. Saddam's effectiveness, at least in political and psychological terms, with something as obsolete as the SCUDs was a reminder of how fast the missiles can travel, and how vulnerable each country is to its neighbors. In the future the missiles will only fly faster.

Epilogue Two:
Russia

IN AUGUST, 1991 THERE WAS A COUP attempt against Mikhail Gorbachev in Moscow. It was a reminder that history does not run in a straight line in Russia. It takes violent turns, it zigs and zags, and for those who get caught leaning the wrong way or thinking the wrong thoughts when history zags, the price can be terrible—not unlike the recent Soviet foreign minister who during the coup against Gorbachev decided to stay out sick. Little school children who are afraid of taking an exam stay out sick from school for a few days but the foreign ministers of powerful police states are not allowed that luxury; they must decide instantly and accurately which way to jump during great crises of history. So the foreign minister becomes the former foreign minister, passing into history even as the rest of the world was still awkwardly learning how to spell and pronounce his name.

Only once before in this century has history moved so swiftly in Russia and that was in 1917. Now the map changes before our eyes. The Baltic Republics have been freed and liberated; Lithuania, Latvia and Estonia are separate and independent nations again. (In the case of Lithuania, a source of much athletic talent, it means the effective demise of Soviet rowing teams and basketball teams.)

Leningrad has become St. Petersburg again. In no other nation do the past and the present struggle so fiercely, and does the name of a city or a street reflect which version of history is winning. No other nation has a greater tendency to obliterate one definition of history for another more favored by its temporary office holders. In other countries, different and conflicting versions of history compete with each other for the attention of the serious scholars; in other countries history is, like life itself, something of a matter of personal choice—in the Soviet Union it has been like many other things, a matter of decree. In Russia it is all or nothing. It is a nation which chooses at each moment to have only a politically correct history. For some fifty years Joseph Stalin dominated Soviet textbooks; now he is in danger of becoming the invisible dictator.

The long volatile Russian summer of 1991 is over. The KGB and the military, the forces of reaction, tried their coup, put Gorbachev under house arrest and then failed; the ghosts of Joseph Stalin and Lavrenti Beria do not smile at this; in the old days when the KGB wanted to destroy a person, or a country, nothing stood in its way. The new generation is not made of stern stuff. In many quarters there is nostalgia for the good old days when the Kremlin's rulers could send tanks into Hungary to subdue a legitimate uprising without fear of reprisal and without being seen live and in color both in the West and at home. Today's KGB people, today's leadership has been contaminated by public opinion, and even worse, the decadent public opinion of the West—part of the price of dealing economically with the West and of coming to the West, hat in hand, asking for economic aid. If Gorbachev was the first Soviet leader to exploit modern Western communications there was a price to that; in the process, the Soviets became at least partially dependent upon the opinion of others in the industrialized world. One of the things that modern communications brings, however involuntarily, is the coming of a different dimension of national conscience, an awareness that others outside the narrow halls of the Kremlin are watching. It becomes harder for the secret police of a nation which wants to be taken seriously by its neighbors, to pull off people's fingernails.

So Leningrad is St. Petersburg again. Gone too is the statue to Felix Dzerzhinsky, the first great figure of the Soviet secret police whose statue in Red Square has been torn down. What other modern nation would so honor and celebrate the head of its secret police, build a giant statue so that millions of its citizens could visit and pay homage to the man who started the tradition of bugging and spying on ordinary citizens, listening to their phones, opening their mail, encouraging them to betray their neighbors, and helping to send them off to the Gulags. That a man who initiated so much evil could have a statue built in his honor and that the statue could last for so long, tells as much about the regime which has just fallen as many of the brilliant history books which are most surely soon to come.

In the past two months events in Russia have outstripped the imagination, and as such are beyond prediction. The summer began with Gorbachev flirting with the Western foreign ministers. If he did not get exactly what he wanted from Bush and the others, the flirt was essentially successful. It was like most things of this sort—as much blackmail as love. What he was really saying, it seemed to me, was in essence; if you do not help me, and if you do not give me what I want, and help strengthen me against my enemies, you will get something far worse. As such that made him the first of the new breed Russian leaders. The old generation, Stalin, the cruelest of all, and even the far more likeable Khrushchev (coming to the UN and banging the table with his shoes and threatening to bury the West), threatened the West by means of force—hundreds of divisions of the Red Army, placed in the center of Europe in Stalin's case, and intercontinental ballistic missiles with nuclear warheads in Khrushchev's.

The new generation, Gorbachev and Yeltsin, threaten us with their weakness, with the idea that we may get something worse. That if we do not help them the country will completely unravel, and it will be our responsibility in the West to deal with it, not theirs in the East to prevent it. What they offer us in effect is a Soviet version of Germany between World War I and World War II, with a Russian

Hitler rising to power. In effect they have been saying: we are so weak we cannot be responsible for our actions, therefore you in the West are responsible for them.

If that was the beginning of the summer, then the moment in August when the coup took place was the highlight. One moment the coup had taken place and Gorbachev had fallen, the next it was all uncertain; perhaps the coup had not completely succeeded, for there was Yeltsin (much denigrated in America, for the decision in elite circles made early in the Gorbachev regime was that Gorbachev was a *good* new generation leader, and that Yeltsin, perceived as cruder and more boorish, and less trustworthy, was a *bad* new generation Russian leader) standing virtually alone against the plotters. This was at first perplexing in much of the outside world since, by all rights in the script, Yeltsin was considered unreliable, and potentially demagogic. And yet there he was being a hero, standing alone against the vast force arrayed against him.

The mistake here is not in the event but in the perception. It is a mistake, I suspect, to envision Russia and to think in terms of good guys and bad guys, and to see Russia in our terms and through our definitions. Before the coup Americans liked Gorbachev and distrusted Yeltsin who was said to be crude, a boor, a drinker, and a womanizer. Gorbachev until then had been the hero of change. In the hours which followed the start of the coup, with Gorbachev under house arrest and quite possibly near death, it was Yeltsin who behaved like the hero of many an American cowboy film and who played the John Wayne role. He defied the coup makers, stood alone, was remarkably courageous, invited a blonde starlet of American television in for an in-the-bunker exclusive television interview, made sure that the Soviet Union was connected to the rest of the wired world and outbluffed the coup makers. Essentially he took the dark techniques that had worked for so long in a totalitarian country and exposed them to the sunlight of international opinion, and for each hour he held out, and for each hour that the rest of the world was a witness, the forces allied against him became weaker.

In those critical first seventy-two hours he did everything right, he saved his principal rival, he fended off tanks, and he touched powerful chords in both domestic and world opinion. He stood off the coup and helped break it, and in those few days it was as if he were magically touched—he was a hero for everyman. Gorbachev, by contrast seemed dazed by the experience, stunned that the coup had been attempted by the very people he had put in power. If there was ever a moment in which a system died it was when Gorbachev returned to Moscow, and Yeltsin and his people forced him to sit at the Soviet tribunal as they read aloud from the secret minutes of the coup what his very own people had done and how they had voted during the coup. It was a political humiliation of the ultimate sort and it was the third of that magnitude which he had suffered within a week; first he had been humiliated by the coup, then by the fact that his rival had saved him, and then once again by the public record of those whom he had promoted and who had betrayed him. He was the man who had done so much to unleash new forces in the Soviet Union but who now was overtaken by the very forces he had unleashed. He was the straddler, the man caught in the middle between the old Russia and the new—one foot in either camp—up to then deftly negotiating; a few months as the hero of the new forces, and then as the old guard became angry, a few months back with them, crushing the Baltic republics for example as a bone to the conservatives, and then after that, mollifying the new forces (and his new friends in the West) by being liberal again. He had straddled in the beginning when it was merely a breach and now it was a chasm and he could straddle no more.

As he sat there in Moscow almost paralyzed by the events (a man of too little faith in the very forces he himself had set free), and Yeltsin seemed by contrast ever more charismatic, I thought of the danger of sitting in a distant democracy and thinking in simplistic Western terms, of good Gorbies and bad Borises, or bad Yeltsinites, and good Gorbyites. For in truth at this moment we know precious little about the two leaders themselves, about the forces they represent, or the forces they must now contend with, and, most important of all, the way that their own population will react to this most precious moment of finally sampling (and being responsible for) the freedoms enjoyed in other parts of the world. What even the most informed writers and commentators on Russia say no longer matters, for they do not know any more than the players in this drama themselves know. Events have outstripped predictions. Everyone now is on virgin territory, everyone is a pioneer. Each day is a surprise.

Neither Gorbachev nor Yeltsin is a man of democracy; each came to power under a brutal totalitarian system. Each is still more given to handing out *decrees* than negotiating in any embryonic democratic form. Democracy, one senses, is for both of them, a form of government in which they and their followers can rule and dominate others, not a form of pluralism which incorporates many forces and in which they on occasion win and on occasion lose. Neither has risen to power based on his ability to listen to people less powerful than himself.

That having been said, this would seem like the key moment to watch which way Russia, or what remains of the Soviet Union, will turn and which path it will follow. The West and the other developed powers wait anxiously for the signs that there are deep and broad democratic stirrings in Russia, that it too will move, however slowly, towards some form of capitalist democracy. When comparable revolutions took place in recent months in Poland, Czechoslovakia, and Hungary, there was little doubt which way their people would force their new governments to go—the course might be hard, the mutation from totalitarianism to democracy clumsy and uneven, but there was a sense of great longing on the part of ordinary people to become a part of something which had been denied to them for so long; to have the most elemental things which are part in the West of what is considered the good life, to be a part of what in America, Japan, and Western Europe could be called the century of the common man.

In that desire there is an essential covenant. The citizen or worker assumes certain obligations in the work place, he works hard, he accepts the disciplines which go with his job, and which have been evolving in various industrialized societies for most of this century (and which vary country by country, but which in the end are also, country by country more similar than dissimilar). In the end if the country has an economy and a political system which are properly tuned there is a trade off; the citizen becomes a voter and a worker and a consumer, and he gets the fruits of the modern industrial society, a decent job with protection from the inequities and potential cruelties of untempered capitalism, decent housing, eventually a car, solid food and a fair chance for a university education for his children. Freedoms exist for both worker and for employer, countervailing rights, the right of the worker to strike, the right of the employer to produce a product are constantly and delicately balanced; above all, the concept depends on the element of freedom of choice—both sides, worker and employer, are given that.

That is the modern definition of the revolution of the common man. It began earlier in this century when the first Henry Ford invented the Model T, and in time the worker became not only a worker but a consumer as well. As part of the revolution, he trades hard work and a sense of obligation for an acceptable amount of fruit for his labor—and protection. In time this revolution produces a balanced and reasonably just state, one which moves ahead through good and bad economic times with a minimum amount of shock and with a marginal amount of social violence. The purpose of the society—a decent and steadily improving standard of living, a chance in one generation to live a better life than that of your parents—is self evident. Individual rights are balanced against those of the state, and the two are constantly negotiated. The state or the government is not all-powerful. That revolution has spread from America to Western Europe and then to Japan and now most recently to Korea and the Little Tigers, and almost surely, the embryonic beginnings already exist in Eastern Europe where the essential concept has already been welcomed.

All of this is alien to Russia. It was a nation which resisted all the implications of political and economic democracy, a nation which lived by decree and by diktat; in an American or a Japanese factory a shoe manufacturer has had to make all sizes and shapes and styles of shoes, but in the Soviet Union the shoe manufacturer made shoes which fit only himself. In America or Japan or West Germany a college graduate could live and work wherever he pleased; in the Soviet Union the state could assign the graduate to a city, and to a job. It was a world where someone was always giving orders and because of that it was a world where it was all right, covertly, to defy the orders, to resist passively, to do deliberately as poor a job as possible at work, while pretending to work. The failure to perform at the workplace was like stealing, but in the mind of the worker it was not stealing because he was withholding his work from the state which did not deserve his work in the first place. Elsewhere the democratic covenants worked; in the Soviet Union, because everything was so authoritarian, it was natural, indeed normal, to cheat and steal.

The idea then of transplanting to Russian soil these ideas, these covenants which have worked so well elsewhere and which depend upon the acceptance and cooperation of the worker, is an intriguing one. Will the system which has worked so well elsewhere work there? Will the covenants hold? Is there enough of a tradition of individual responsibility to give the nation a beginning of modernization? Or have expectations and a sense of entitlement already exceeded the reality of the amount of obligation required. Do people there expect democracy to work instantly, and by democracy do they envision a society where they have greater personal freedom, but where the state assumes as much obligation as ever to take care of them in case things do not work out? Do they assume that the most critical aspect of all of industrial middle-class democracy, the economic underpinnings, are theirs by right?

No one knows. This is a nation which in any real sense has been off the map of Europe for most of its history. It is connected to

Europe, but it is not *of* Europe. The industrial revolution never reached that far east. The government of the Czar fell so readily to the Communists because the country was so backward, the underpinnings so vulnerable, the core of the society so feudal (and made even more vulnerable by the immense drain of World War I). The complicated balance of forces which make an industrialized nation coherent, a blend which permits the energy of the nation to be used, and keeps one force from obliterating others is not something easily achieved; nor does it come from revolution. Rather it evolves, a product of a nation's history and its culture, an acceptance of modernization, a societal view toward itself and toward the outside world which is reasonably honest. Those ingredients have always been missing in Russia.

When I was a young reporter working in Eastern Europe as a correspondent, I had a sense that, although officially the nations were Communist—as decreed by the map drawn by the successes of the Red Army—their souls were capitalist, that the real economy was a black market economy, and that to get anything done, you had to use the black market. Thus, Communism was simply a temporary handicap imposed on them by the Red Army. The people themselves longed to work, to barter, to have hard currency and to make choices, and to have the good life as enjoyed elsewhere in the West. They knew the good life existed, they could tell from the American movies they watched. The Communist government carefully censored the movies, of course, showing only those which were judged to be critical of capitalism; but the shrewd citizens of Poland and Czechoslovakia were never looking at the story per se, they were watching for the background, and they could tell, even in a movie allegedly critical of capitalism, that everyone in America was better dressed, better fed, better housed, and tended to own a car. (Comparably, when I was working in Eastern Europe in the mid-1960s, a black group announced a protest of the World's Fair being held then in New York and this was much publicized by the Communist press; all the blacks in the group would park their cars blocking the various bridges leading to the Fair. In Eastern Europe, where ownership of a car was the sign of a very rich man, the fact that blacks owned cars, and could protest capitalism by parking them illegally was a source of great amusement.) The people of Eastern Europe understood the essential covenant of the West and longed to be a part of it.

About Russia I am not so sure. No one really knows yet. Clearly for most Russians over the age of thirty or thirty-five it will be hard to make a new start. For those who have lived too long under the total state ambitions are dampened; their expectation is that the state, even if you despise it, will somehow take care of you, and will deliver, however incompetently and behind schedule, bad food, a bad apartment, a bad job—it may not be much, but it suffices. In the process there is no doubt that a great deal of damage has been done to any acceptance of individual ambition.

But my reservations about the future of Russia go far beyond this. That which we in the industrialized world have come to think of in broad terms as a kind of social, political, and cultural enlightenment has never touched Russia. It is not just that Russia has been separated from Europe for some seventy years, it is that it has been separated from it for hundreds of years, and it is a sense that there is something dark and angry and suspicious about the nation, a cumulative attitude towards others which makes acceptance of the democratic covenant difficult. It is a peasant nation, burdened for centuries by a peasant resistance to authority, a peasant resistance to learning, and a peasant resistance to modernization.

It has evolved this way for complicated reasons. Part of the reason is geography, so far from the center of Europe. Part of it is size and diversity; it is a hard country to govern, because a central authority is always distant and because the varying parts of it are so disparate. Part of the problem is a powerful church that seems to resist the modernization which the churches, in nations which have been industrially successful, have not resisted, but have in fact aided. It is not surprising that the most articulate of Communism's critics, Alexander Solzhenitsyn, was a man who hated the regime, hated the gulag, and hated the West, which he found decadent. He had little curiosity about America, where he lived, and he isolated himself and created in Vermont a small Russia in his own image; in the process he had no idea at all of the pluralism and the richness and the diversity of the nation around him. He saw the seamy unspeakable side of New York City and decided that all of the West was decadent. All around him in Vermont was the traditional piety of a small New England village and he never comprehended it. His vision of the new Russia was not merely to end Communism—a worthy ambition indeed, particularly for so brilliant a man who had suffered so long and so hard under it and who had so skillfully recorded its horrors—but it often seemed, to return it to a fifteenth century church-dominated theocracy.

That anger and that resistance to modernity, and indeed that selfishness are still there. No country over the last century has done so systematic a job of destroying its middle class, and thereby retarding its own growth and development. In Japan a form of government, which is best described as communal capitalism, succeeded, and in Russia a communal socialism failed; this happened in part because capitalism is a far more logical economic system, offering all participants in the system incremental shares of reward, and communism is a system which offered no incentive at all. But it happened as well, I suspect, because the Japanese were determined to make their form of government succeed, and it is even possible, given the economic abilities of the Japanese that they would have done the truly impossible, and made some form of communism work.

The question then is whether in Russia there can be modern industrial covenants which work and which are like those in other modern states, or whether the resentments and the prejudices are too strong, the darkness too great, the instinct to *resist* (and to resist anything, any force, any government) too Pavlovian. A high Russian economic minister under Gorbachev told a friend of mine, in the West, if your neighbor has a nice house then you want to work hard to have one like it; here, he added, if your neighbor has a lovely house then you want to burn it down. Already, given the rise in entrepreneurial capitalism in Russia there is a class of new rich, of Russian millionaires and as here they have become immediately vulnerable to the rawest kind of crime and have begun forming groups to protect themselves. What is bothersome to those who visit Russia is the harshness of the place, the instinct on the part of ordinary people to resist accepting responsibility for events, and to blame events on others.

The easy assumption about the Soviet Union in the past was that it was a terrible and brutalized place because Joseph Stalin was so sinister and brutal a figure; but there is also a school of thought that Stalin was that harsh and brutal a figure because as a Russian peasant he knew the other peasants and knew what it would take to subdue them and to force them to obey his will. Brutality, in that thesis, begot brutality. Darkness begot even more darkness. The system was vicious because the men who authored it knew their own people and thought nothing else would work.

Will the sense of obligation meet that of the sense of entitlement? In the past this was a nation burdened on its way into the modern century by a harsh repressive totalitarian government. Now that that cruel and self-destructive government is finally being removed, will we find that it was burdened even more deeply by its own culture as well, that the repressiveness was merely an extension of the culture?

Epilogue Three:
America

A FOUNDATION IN AMERICA RECENTLY participated in the testing of children from seven countries, ages thirteen and fourteen years old, in math and science. The young people were from the developed countries, and some newly developing ones. Not surprisingly, the Japanese and Korean children recorded the highest scores. Again, not surprisingly, the American children were at the bottom. The children were also asked how well they *thought* they had done. The results showed that the American children thought they had done the best of all.